International recommendations
on labour statistics

International recommendations on labour statistics

International Labour Office · Geneva

ISBN 92-2-101376-6

First published 1976

331·0182

24 APR 1978

Printed by Imprimeries Populaires, Geneva, Switzerland

CONTENTS

Text:

INTRODUCTION

For more than 50 years the International Labour Organisation has been methodically engaging in the task of standardising labour statistics.

That task has been carried out by the International Labour Office principally through the organisation of international conferences of labour statisticians, of which there have been 12 up to the present. These conferences, in which all the States Members of the Organisation may take part, bring together experts appointed by the governments, most of whom are officials of government departments. Their formal conclusions are expressed in resolutions submitted for approval to the Governing Body of the International Labour Office.[1]

Since several other international organisations, including in particular the United Nations, are also interested in the standardisation of labour statistics, a system of close collaboration has been established in this field.

One of the fruits of that collaboration has been the gradual building up of a body of guidelines relating to the methodology of labour statistics. The purpose of this publication [2] is to present systematically the main recommendations that are at present in effect.

These recommendations are set out according to the subject-matter of the labour statistics to which they refer in ten chapters, all of which follow the same plan. In each chapter there is an opening section in which the work done under the auspices of the ILO or other international organisations is briefly recapitulated. The work accomplished at conferences, including especially the International Conferences of Labour Statisticians, and at committees and

---

[1] The subjects that were examined at the 12 International Conferences of Labour Statisticians are listed in the Appendix.

[2] The present publication replaces the one published in 1959 under the title of *The international standardisation of labour statistics*, Studies and reports, New series, No. 53 (Geneva, ILO).

meetings of experts that have been convened over the years was prepared in many technical studies and resulted in a series of reports. A selection of this material, which constitutes an important source of information and of guidance for international action, is given in a second section containing a list of references. As for the recommendations themselves, they are reproduced in a third section of each chapter.

As already mentioned, only the principal recommendations relating to labour statistics are considered. There are also many other international recommendations relating to other subjects or to other branches of statistics that also have a bearing on labour statistics. They include, in particular, the recommendations of the Statistical Commission of the United Nations, especially those relating to national accounts and the complementary system of statistics on distribution of income, consumption and accumulation, those relating to censuses of population and housing and to industrial statistics and also those that will appear in the future system of social and demographic statistics.

It should be borne in mind, too, that statistical methods are constantly evolving. In the field of data processing, the advances that have been made open up new horizons that would have been unimaginable only 10 or 20 years ago. The recommendations set out in the present publication none the less do provide a solid body of internationally approved guidelines that should be followed in the organisation, development and improvement of systems of labour statistics, especially in the developing countries.

MAJOR ECONOMIC CLASSIFICATIONS

1

The three classifications considered here—industrial, occupational and by status—are of fundamental importance in labour statistics. Especially for purposes of international comparison, it is desirable that the data available in the various countries be classified or organised along similar lines.

CLASSIFICATION OF INDUSTRIES

It was in 1923, at the First International Conference of Labour Statisticians, that the classification of industries and occupations was first considered. The question had been the subject of a preparatory study in which the ILO had summarised the classifications in use in a number of countries and presented the principles underlying the different uses of the proposed international classification [1].[1] In its resolution, the Conference emphasised the distinction between classification by industry and classification by occupation, pointing out that, for purposes of classifying the labour force, the primary classification should be according to industries, and it drew up a list of main divisions of economic activity: primary production (e.g. agriculture and mining), secondary production (manufacturing and construction) and services (e.g. transport, commerce and administration) [2].

In 1925 and 1926 the Second and Third International Conferences of Labour Statisticians considered again the classification of industries; the Second Conference recommended that the Office draw up a provisional list of the most important industries for use in labour statistics [3] and the Third suggested that the details of the specific content of each industry group as used in the classifications of the different countries be compiled as a further step in the direction of establishing a uniform list [4]. In response to the resolution adopted by the

---

[1] The figures in brackets refer to the studies and reports listed in the second section of each chapter.

Second Conference the Office prepared a provisional list of the principal branches of economic activity to facilitate presentation in a uniform order of the data available in respect of wages, employment and unemployment [5].

The Committee of Statistical Experts of the League of Nations, having been called upon to consider the problem of industrial classification in relation to the gainfully occupied population, was, for its part, to recommend in 1938 the formulation of a uniform definition of the "gainfully employed" and two lists of industries—a minimum list and a more detailed list—with a view to ensuring international comparability of figures [6].

Following the Second World War the question of an international classification by branch of economic activity was taken up anew by the Statistical Commission of the United Nations. A preliminary draft of the classification was submitted to the governments and to the specialised agencies and subsequently revised in the light of the comments received. The classification was adopted by the Statistical Commission in May 1948. In July-August 1948 the Economic and Social Council of the United Nations recommended that the various governments make use of the International Standard Classification of all Economic Activities (ISIC), either by adopting it as a national standard or by rearranging their statistical data in accordance with the classification for purposes of international comparability.

The Classification was revised in some respects in 1958 and again in 1968 [7]. The present version (see "Texts", item A, in the third section of this chapter) takes into account the experience acquired and reflects also the changes that have taken place in the relative importance and in the organisation of various types of economic activity. As a result, its classification structure has four, instead of three, levels.

CLASSIFICATION OF OCCUPATIONS

The desirability and possibility of an international standard classification of occupations was considered in 1923 by the First International Conference of Labour Statisticians [1]. While the Conference recognised the usefulness of a classification of occupations as distinct from a classification of industries, it proposed no formal groupings of occupations [2].

The subject of the classification of occupations was again placed on the agenda of the Seventh International Conference of Labour Statisticians (1949), for which the ILO had prepared a report [8]. The Conference [9] adopted a classification of occupations into nine major groups and suggested a series of basic principles to be followed in the collection and tabulation of the data (see "Texts", item B).

A list of minor groups was submitted in 1954 to the Eighth International Conference of Labour Statisticians [10], which approved provisionally a classification [11] subsequently submitted to the governments and to a group of experts. After making some amendments to the draft submitted to it [12], the Ninth International Conference of Labour Statisticians (1957) adopted the International Standard Classification of Occupations (ISCO), consisting of major, minor and unit groups (three-digit code numbers). The Conference recommended that, for purposes of international comparison, countries reporting statistics on the occupational characteristics of the civilian labour force derived from population censuses and other statistical inquiries of international interest should arrange, as far as possible, for the data to be presented in conformity with the International Classification [13]. This classification, together with definitions of the major, minor and unit groups drafted in consultation with the governments, was published in 1958 [14].

With a view to a revision that had already been proposed by the Ninth International Conference of Labour Statisticians, the ILO collected in 1964 the comments of about 80 countries and ten international organisations concerning the classification. Towards the end of 1965, a working party examined the suggestions received and formulated recommendations [15] that served for the preparation of a draft revision of the classification. The revision was submitted in 1966 to the Eleventh International Conference of Labour Statisticians [16], which adopted a new list of major groups, minor groups and unit groups (see "Texts", item C) [17].

Published in 1969 (English version), the revised edition of the International Standard Classification of Occupations [18] was developed, like its predecessor, to provide a systematic basis for presentation of occupational data relating to different countries in order to facilitate international comparisons. The classification structure has four levels, providing successively finer detail, as follows: major groups (8), minor groups (83), unit groups (284) and occupational categories (1,506) (see "Texts", item D). It includes definitions given for each of the 1,881 titles, in which the general functions of the occupation followed and the main tasks performed by the worker concerned are described. In order to facilitate use of the classification, an expanded alphabetical list of several thousand titles is given in an appendix, as well as a table of conversion from the 1958 classification to the revised classification. A separate document [19] shows, in the order of the code numbers, all the titles given in the Expanded Alphabetical List.

CLASSIFICATION ACCORDING TO STATUS

The first international step towards the classification of workers by status was taken in 1938 by the Committee of Statistical Experts of the League of Nations, which recommended the following classification of the gainfully occupied population: (1) employers (persons working on their own account with paid assistants in their occupation); (2) persons working on their own account either alone or with the assistance of members of their families; (3) members of families aiding the head of their families in his occupation; (4) persons in receipt of salaries or wages.

The Sixth (1947) International Conference of Labour Statisticians [20], in its resolution concerning statistics of employment, unemployment and the labour force, recommended that such statistics should include the following groups, which are very similar to those proposed by the League of Nations (and which were to be taken over in 1954, practically without any change, by the Eighth International Conference of Labour Statisticians): (1) workers for public or private employers; (2) employers; (3) workers who work on their own account without employees; (4) unpaid family workers.

In 1948 the Population Commission of the United Nations recommended that, in censuses, the economically active population be classified according to status into the groups proposed by the Sixth International Conference of Labour Statisticians. In 1950 it adopted standard definitions for these groups.

A further group was added in 1958 in the recommendations concerning population censuses approved by the Statistical Commission of the United Nations—namely, "members of producers' co-operatives". This group covers all persons who are active members of such a co-operative, regardless of the industry in which it is established. In 1966 the same Commission adopted the principles and recommendations for the 1970 population censuses [21], which contain a revised description of the groups constituting the classification according to status (see "Texts", item E).

References

[1] ILO: *Systems of classification of industries and occupations*, Studies and reports, Series N, No. 1 (Geneva, 1923).

[2] — *International Conference of Labour Statisticians*, Studies and reports, Series N, No. 4 (Geneva, 1924), pp. 8-30.

[3] — *The Second International Conference of Labour Statisticians*, Studies and reports, Series N, No. 8 (Geneva, 1925), pp. 40-46.

[4] — *The Third International Conference of Labour Statisticians*, Studies and reports, Series N, No. 12 (Geneva, 1926), pp. 86-91 and 104.

[5] — *International Labour Review*, Sep. 1933, pp. 414-415.

[6] League of Nations: *Statistics of the Gainfully Occupied Population. Definitions and Classifications Recommended by the Committee of Statistical Experts*, Studies and reports on statistical methods, No. 1 (1938, II.A.12) (Geneva, 1938).

[7] United Nations: *International Standard Industrial Classification of All Economic Activities*, Statistical Papers, Series M, No. 4 (Lake Success (New York), 1949), Rev. 1 (New York, 1958) and Rev. 2 (New York, 1968).

[8] ILO: *International standard classification of occupations*, Studies and reports, New series, No. 15 (Geneva, 1949).

[9] — *The Seventh International Conference of Labour Statisticians* (Geneva, 1951), pp. 8-15 and 51-54.

[10] — *International standard classification of occupations: minor groups*, Eighth International Conference of Labour Statisticians, Report II (Geneva, 1954; mimeographed).

[11] — *The Eighth International Conference of Labour Statisticians, 1954* (Geneva, 1955; mimeographed), pp. 8-15 and 49-54.

[12] — *International standard classification of occupations*, Ninth International Conference of Labour Statisticians, Report II (Geneva, 1957; mimeographed).

[13] — *Ninth International Conference of Labour Statisticians, 1957* (Geneva; mimeographed), pp. 17-27 and 58-70.

[14] — *International standard classification of occupations* (Geneva, 1958).

[15] — *Report of the working group on revision of ISCO* (Geneva, doc. WG/ISCO/65/3; mimeographed; 1966).

[16] — *Revision of the international standard classification of occupations*, Eleventh International Conference of Labour Statisticians, Report III and Appendix II to Report III: *Draft definitions* (Geneva, mimeographed; 1966).

[17] — *The Eleventh International Conference of Labour Statisticians, 1966* (Geneva, 1967; mimeographed), pp. 13-23 and 45-55.

[18] — *International standard classification of occupations—revised edition, 1968* (Geneva, 1969).

[19] — *Classified list of codes and titles*, International Standard Classification of Occupations (revised, 1968) (Geneva, 1968).

[20] — *The Sixth International Conference of Labour Statisticians*, Studies and reports, New series, No. 7, Part 4 (Geneva, 1948), p. 55.

[21] United Nations: *Principles and Recommendations for the 1970 Population Censuses*, Statistical papers, Series M, No. 44 (New York, 1967).

Texts

A. International Standard Industrial Classification of all Economic Activities: List of major divisions, divisions, major groups and groups[1]

MAJOR DIVISION 1. AGRICULTURE, HUNTING, FORESTRY AND FISHING

11 Agriculture and hunting
    111 1110 Agricultural and livestock production
    112 1120 Agricultural services
    113 1130 Hunting, trapping and game propagation

12 Forestry and logging
    121 1210 Forestry
    122 1220 Logging

13 130 Fishing
        1301 Ocean and coastal fishing
        1302 Fishing not elsewhere classified

MAJOR DIVISION 2. MINING AND QUARRYING

21 210 2100 Coal mining

---

[1] For the full text of the Classification, including the descriptions of the industries, see United Nations: *International Standard Industrial Classification of All Economic Activities*, Statistical papers, Series M, No. 4, Rev. 2 (New York, 1968).

22 220 2200 Crude petroleum and natural gas production

23 230 Metal ore mining
        2301 Iron ore mining
        2302 Non-ferrous metal ore mining

29 290 Other mining
        2901 Stone quarrying, clay and sand pits
        2902 Chemical and fertiliser mineral mining
        2903 Salt mining
        2909 Mining and quarrying not elsewhere classified

Major Division 3. Manufacturing

31 Manufacture of food, beverages and tobacco
  311–
  312 Food manufacturing
        3111 Slaughtering, preparing and preserving meat
        3112 Manufacture of dairy products
        3113 Canning and preserving of fruits and vegetables
        3114 Canning, preserving and processing of fish, crustacea and similar foods
        3115 Manufacture of vegetable and animal oils and fats
        3116 Grain mill products
        3117 Manufacture of bakery products
        3118 Sugar factories and refineries
        3119 Manufacture of cocoa, chocolate and sugar confectionery
        3121 Manufacture of food products not elsewhere classified
        3122 Manufacture of prepared animal feeds

  313 Beverage industries
        3131 Distilling, rectifying and blending spirits
        3132 Wine industries
        3133 Malt liquors and malt
        3134 Soft drinks and carbonated waters industries

  314 3140 Tobacco manufactures

32 Textile, wearing apparel and leather industries
  321 Manufacture of textiles
        3211 Spinning, weaving and finishing textiles
        3212 Manufacture of made-up textile goods except wearing apparel
        3213 Knitting mills
        3214 Manufacture of carpets and rugs
        3215 Cordage, rope and twine industries
        3219 Manufacture of textiles not elsewhere classified

  322 3220 Manufacture of wearing apparel, except footwear

  323 Manufacture of leather and products of leather, leather substitutes and fur, except footwear and wearing apparel
        3231 Tanneries and leather finishing
        3232 Fur dressing and dyeing industries

3233 Manufacture of products of leather and leather substitutes, except footwear and wearing apparel

324 3240 Manufacture of footwear, except vulcanised or moulded rubber or plastic footwear

33 Manufacture of wood and wood products, including furniture

331 Manufacture of wood and wood and cork products, except furniture
3311 Sawmills, planing and other wood mills
3312 Manufacture of wooden and cane containers and small cane ware
3319 Manufacture of wood and cork products not elsewhere classified

332 3320 Manufacture of furniture and fixtures, except primarily of metal

34 Manufacture of paper and paper products; printing and publishing

341 Manufacture of paper and paper products
3411 Manufacture of pulp, paper and paperboard
3412 Manufacture of containers and boxes of paper and paperboard
3419 Manufacture of pulp, paper and paperboard articles not elsewhere classified

342 3420 Printing, publishing and allied industries

35 Manufacture of chemicals and chemical, petroleum, coal, rubber and plastic products

351 Manufacture of industrial chemicals
3511 Manufacture of basic industrial chemicals except fertiliser
3512 Manufacture of fertilisers and pesticides
3513 Manufacture of synthetic resins, plastic materials and man-made fibres except glass

352 Manufacture of other chemical products
3521 Manufacture of paints, varnishes and lacquers
3522 Manufacture of drugs and medicines
3523 Manufacture of soap and cleaning preparations, perfumes, cosmetics and other toilet preparations
3529 Manufacture of chemical products not elsewhere classified

353 3530 Petroleum refineries

354 3540 Manufacture of miscellaneous products of petroleum and coal

355 Manufacture of rubber products
3551 Tyre and tube industries
3559 Manufacture of rubber products not elsewhere classified

356 3560 Manufacture of plastic products not elsewhere classified

36 Manufacture of non-metallic mineral products, except products of petroleum and coal

361 3610 Manufacture of pottery, china and earthenware

362 3620 Manufacture of glass and glass products

369 Manufacture of other non-metallic mineral products
3691 Manufacture of structural clay products
3692 Manufacture of cement, lime and plaster
3699 Manufacture of non-metallic mineral products not elsewhere classified

37 Basic metal industries

    371   3710   Iron and steel basic industries

    372   3720   Non-ferrous metal basic industries

38 Manufacture of fabricated metal products, machinery and equipment

    381   Manufacture of fabricated metal products, except machinery and equipment

        3811   Manufacture of cutlery, hand tools and general hardware
        3812   Manufacture of furnitures and fixtures primarily of metal
        3813   Manufacture of structural metal products
        3819   Manufacture of fabricated metal products except machinery and equipment not elsewhere classified

    382   Manufacture of machinery except electrical

        3821   Manufacture of engines and turbines
        3822   Manufacture of agricultural machinery and equipment
        3823   Manufacture of metal and wood working machinery
        3824   Manufacture of special industrial machinery and equipment except metal and wood working machinery
        3825   Manufacture of office, computing and accounting machinery
        3829   Machinery and equipment except electrical not elsewhere classified

    383   Manufacture of electrical machinery apparatus, appliances and supplies

        3831   Manufacture of electrical industrial machinery and apparatus
        3832   Manufacture of radio, television and communication equipment and apparatus
        3833   Manufacture of electrical appliances and housewares
        3839   Manufacture of electrical apparatus and supplies not elsewhere classified

    384   Manufacture of transport equipment

        3841   Shipbuilding and repairing
        3842   Manufacture of railroad equipment
        3843   Manufacture of motor vehicles
        3844   Manufacture of motorcycles and bicycles
        3845   Manufacture of aircraft
        3849   Manufacture of transport equipment not elsewhere classified

    385   Manufacture of professional and scientific and measuring and controlling equipment not elsewhere classified, and of photographic and optical goods

        3851   Manufacture of professional and scientific and measuring and controlling equipment not elsewhere classified
        3852   Manufacture of photographic and optical goods
        3853   Manufacture of watches and clocks

39 390 Other manufacturing industries

        3901   Manufacture of jewellery and related articles
        3902   Manufacture of musical instruments
        3903   Manufacture of sporting and athletic goods
        3909   Manufacturing industries not elsewhere classified

MAJOR DIVISION 4. ELECTRICITY, GAS AND WATER

41 410 Electricity, gas and steam

        4101   Electric light and power

		4102	Gas manufacture and distribution
		4103	Steam and hot water supply
42	420	4200	Water works and supply

MAJOR DIVISION 5. CONSTRUCTION

50	500	5000	Construction

MAJOR DIVISION 6. WHOLESALE AND RETAIL TRADE
AND RESTAURANTS AND HOTELS

61	610	6100	Wholesale trade

62	620	6200	Retail trade

63 Restaurants and hotels

	631	6310	Restaurants, cafés and other eating and drinking places
	632	6320	Hotels, rooming houses, camps and other lodging places

MAJOR DIVISION 7. TRANSPORT, STORAGE AND COMMUNICATION

71 Transport and storage

    711 Land transport

        7111 Railway transport
        7112 Urban, suburban and inter-urban highway passenger transport
        7113 Other passenger land transport
        7114 Freight transport by road
        7115 Pipeline transport
        7116 Supporting services to land transport

    712 Water transport

        7121 Ocean and coastal water transport
        7122 Inland water transport
        7123 Supporting services to water transport

    713 Air transport

        7131 Air transport carriers
        7132 Supporting services to air transport

    719 Services allied to transport

        7191 Services incidental to transport
        7192 Storage and warehousing

72	720	7200	Communication

MAJOR DIVISION 8. FINANCING, INSURANCE, REAL ESTATE AND BUSINESS SERVICES

81 810 Financial institutions

        8101 Monetary institutions
        8102 Other financial institutions
        8103 Financial services

82	820	8200	Insurance

83 Real estate and business services

    831 8310 Real estate

832 Business services except machinery and equipment rental and leasing
  8321 Legal services
  8322 Accounting, auditing and bookkeeping services
  8323 Data processing and tabulating services
  8324 Engineering, architectural and technical services
  8325 Advertising services
  8329 Business services, except machinery and equipment rental and leasing, not elsewhere classified

833 8330 Machinery and equipment rental and leasing

Major Division 9. Community, Social and Personal Services

91 910 9100 Public administration and defence

92 920 9200 Sanitary and similar services

93 Social and related community services
  931 9310 Education services
  932 9320 Research and scientific institutes
  933 Medical, dental, other health and veterinary services
    9331 Medical, dental and other health services
    9332 Veterinary services
  934 9340 Welfare institutions
  935 9350 Business, professional and labour associations
  939 Other social and related community services
    9391 Religious organisations
    9399 Social and related community services not elsewhere classified

94 Recreational and cultural services
  941 Motion picture and other entertainment services
    9411 Motion picture production
    9412 Motion picture distribution and projection
    9413 Radio and television broadcasting
    9414 Theatrical producers and entertainment services
    9415 Authors, music composers, and other independent artists not elsewhere classified
  942 9420 Libraries, museums, botanical and zoological gardens, and other cultural services not elsewhere classified
  949 9490 Amusement and recreational services not elsewhere classified

95 Personal and household services
  951 Repair services not elsewhere classified
    9511 Repair of footwear and other leather goods
    9512 Electrical repair shops
    9513 Repair of motor vehicles and motorcycles
    9514 Watch, clock and jewellery repair
    9519 Other repair shops not elsewhere classified
  952 9520 Laundries, laundry services, and cleaning and dyeing plants
  953 9530 Domestic services

959 Miscellaneous personal services
    9591 Barber and beauty shops
    9592 Photographic studios, including commercial photography
    9599 Personal services not elsewhere classified

96 960 9600 International and Other Extra-Territorial Bodies

MAJOR DIVISION 0. ACTIVITIES NOT ADEQUATELY DEFINED

0 000 0000 Activities not adequately defined.

B. International Standard Classification of Occupations: Resolution adopted by the Seventh International Conference of Labour Statisticians (September-October 1949)

. . . .

1. Each country should classify its civilian labour force, as shown by its population censuses, according to occupational groups, as well as according to industrial status and industry.

. . . .

3. *(a)* The basis of any classification of occupations should be the trade, profession or type of work performed by the individual, irrespective of the branch of economic activity to which he is attached or of his industrial status.

(b) Proprietors or owners who mainly perform the same work as that performed by employees in their own or in a similar enterprise should be allocated to the same group to which the employees are allocated.

4. Since many of the problems encountered in the classification of individuals according to their occupation are due to the vagueness or insufficiency of the information furnished, particular attention should be paid to the formulation of the questions referring to the occupation, and to obtaining the full information needed to identify the occupation: for example, answers such as employer, owner, proprietor, foreman, worker, employee, where given, should be supplemented with information as to the actual kind of work performed.

5. In order to ascertain clearly the occupation of an individual, information on industrial status and industry should always be collected simultaneously with that on the occupation itself.

. . . .

C. International Standard Classification of Occupations: Resolution adopted by the Eleventh International Conference of Labour Statisticians (October 1966)

The Eleventh International Conference of Labour Statisticians,

. . . .

Considering that, in connection with preparations for the censuses of population to be taken in or around 1970, a revised edition of the International Standard Classification of Occupations should be published as soon as possible;

Considering also that further development and improvement of the International Standard Classification of Occupations will assist in promoting the international comparability of statistics derived from sources other than population censuses;

Recalling the recommendations of the Seventh, Eighth and Ninth International Conferences of Labour Statisticians establishing the principles on which the International Standard Classification of Occupations should be based and, in particular, the resolution of the Ninth Conference endorsing the major, minor and unit groups of the existing standard classification;

Recalling also that the resolution of the Ninth Conference provided that proposals for amendments to the International Standard Classification of Occupations which may be submitted by governments, or which appear to be necessary on the basis of experience in practical application of the classification, should be considered by an International Conference of Labour Statisticians after the results of the population censuses taken in or around 1960 were available,

Adopts, this twenty-eighth day of October 1966, the following resolution:

1. The occupational classification system of major, minor and unit groups shown in the annex to this resolution [1] is endorsed by the Conference and is designated the International Standard Classification of Occupations, 1966 (ISCO 1966).

2. In reporting, for purposes of international comparisons, statistics on the occupational characteristics of persons in the civilian labour force, derived from censuses of population or other statistical inquiries, each country should supply data in conformity with ISCO, so far as possible.

3. Each country should make available to the International Labour Office, in respect of the classification (or classifications) used for national statistical purposes, a list (or lists) of the occupational groups which it considers to be within the scope of each major, minor and unit group of ISCO, as far as possible.

4. In view of the changes in occupations, particularly as a result of technological development, and also of the evolution in methods of collecting, analysing and utilising occupation information, it is essential that continuing research and development work on occupational classification be carried out. In this connection information on these matters should be collected and disseminated.

5. Work should begin at an early date on a further revision of the International Standard Classification of Occupations. This revision should be completed as soon as possible after the results of the 1970 censuses become available. Account should be taken of experience with the use of the International Standard Classification of Occupations in connection with the population censuses and also of experience which will have been acquired in the use of the International Standard Classification of Occupations for other purposes during the next few years. In this connection the work on the revision should be phased over a sufficiently long period to allow for adequate consultations with governments, organisations of employers and workers and of other interested organisations and individuals. In carrying out the revision, full recognition should be given to both the statistical and non-statistical applications of the International Standard Classification of Occupations.

. . . .

D. International Standard Classification of Occupations: List of Major, Minor and Unit Groups [2]

MAJOR GROUP 0/1: PROFESSIONAL, TECHNICAL AND RELATED WORKERS

0-1 Physical scientists and related technicians

    0-11 Chemists
    0-12 Physicists
    0-13 Physical scientists not elsewhere classified
    0-14 Physical science technicians

---

[1] See below, Text D.

[2] For the full text of the Classification, including the titles and definitions of the occupations, see ILO: *International standard classification of occupations—revised edition, 1968* (Geneva, 1969).

0-2/0-3   Architects, engineers and related technicians
- 0-21   Architects and town planners
- 0-22   Civil engineers
- 0-23   Electrical and electronics engineers
- 0-24   Mechanical engineers
- 0-25   Chemical engineers
- 0-26   Metallurgists
- 0-27   Mining engineers
- 0-28   Industrial engineers
- 0-29   Engineers not elsewhere classified
- 0-31   Surveyors
- 0-32   Draughtsmen
- 0-33   Civil engineering technicians
- 0-34   Electrical and electronic engineering technicians
- 0-35   Mechanical engineering technicians
- 0-36   Chemical engineering technicians
- 0-37   Metallurgical technicians
- 0-38   Mining technicians
- 0-39   Engineering technicians not elsewhere classified

0-4   Aircraft and ships' officers
- 0-41   Aircraft pilots, navigators and flight engineers
- 0-42   Ships' deck officers and pilots
- 0-43   Ships' engineers

0-5   Life scientists and related technicians
- 0-51   Biologists, zoologists and related scientists
- 0-52   Bacteriologists, pharmacologists and related scientists
- 0-53   Agronomists and related scientists
- 0-54   Life sciences technicians

0-6/0-7   Medical, dental, veterinary and related workers
- 0-61   Medical doctors
- 0-62   Medical assistants
- 0-63   Dentists
- 0-64   Dental assistants
- 0-65   Veterinarians
- 0-66   Veterinary assistants
- 0-67   Pharmacists
- 0-68   Pharmaceutical assistants
- 0-69   Dieticians and public health nutritionists
- 0-71   Professional nurses
- 0-72   Nursing personnel not elsewhere classified
- 0-73   Professional midwives
- 0-74   Midwifery personnel not elsewhere classified
- 0-75   Optometrists and opticians
- 0-76   Physiotherapists and occupational therapists
- 0-77   Medical X-ray technicians
- 0-79   Medical, dental, veterinary and related workers not elsewhere classified

0-8   Statisticians, mathematicians, systems analysts and related technicians
- 0-81   Statisticians
- 0-82   Mathematicians and actuaries
- 0-83   Systems analysts
- 0-84   Statistical and mathematical technicians

0-9 Economists

    0-90 Economists

1-1 Accountants

    1-10 Accountants

1-2 Jurists

    1-21 Lawyers
    1-22 Judges
    1-29 Jurists not elsewhere classified

1-3 Teachers

    1-31 University and higher education teachers
    1-32 Secondary education teachers
    1-33 Primary education teachers
    1-34 Pre-primary education teachers
    1-35 Special education teachers
    1-39 Teachers not elsewhere classified

1-4 Workers in religion

    1-41 Ministers of religion and related members of religious orders
    1-49 Workers in religion not elsewhere classified

1-5 Authors, journalists and related writers

    1-51 Authors and critics
    1-59 Authors, journalists and related writers not elsewhere classified

1-6 Sculptors, painters, photographers and related creative artists

    1-61 Sculptors, painters and related artists
    1-62 Commercial artists and designers
    1-63 Photographers and cameramen

1-7 Composers and performing artists

    1-71 Composers, musicians and singers
    1-72 Choreographers and dancers
    1-73 Actors and stage directors
    1-74 Producers (performing arts)
    1-75 Circus performers
    1-79 Performing artists not elsewhere classified

1-8 Athletes, sportsmen and related workers

    1-80 Athletes, sportsmen and related workers

1-9 Professional and technical workers not elsewhere classified

    1-91 Librarians, archivists and curators
    1-92 Sociologists, anthropologists and related scientists
    1-93 Social workers
    1-94 Personnel and occupational specialists
    1-95 Philologists, translators and interpreters
    1-99 Other professional and technical workers

MAJOR GROUP 2: ADMINISTRATIVE AND MANAGERIAL WORKERS

2-0 Legislative officials and government administrators

    2-01 Legislative officials
    2-02 Government administrators

2-1 Managers
    2-11 General managers
    2-12 Production managers (except farm)
    2-19 Managers not elsewhere classified

MAJOR GROUP 3: CLERICAL AND RELATED WORKERS

3-0 Clerical supervisors
    3-00 Clerical supervisors

3-1 Government executive officials
    3-10 Government executive officials

3-2 Stenographers, typists and card and tape punching machine operators
    3-21 Stenographers, typists and teletypists
    3-22 Card and tape punching machine operators

3-3 Bookkeepers, cashiers and related workers
    3-31 Bookkeepers and cashiers
    3-39 Bookkeepers, cashiers and related workers not elsewhere classified

3-4 Computing machine operators
    3-41 Bookkeeping and calculating machine operators
    3-42 Automatic data processing machine operators

3-5 Transport and communications supervisors
    3-51 Railway station masters
    3-52 Postmasters
    3-59 Transport and communications supervisors not elsewhere classified

3-6 Transport conductors
    3-60 Transport conductors

3-7 Mail distribution clerks
    3-70 Mail distribution clerks

3-8 Telephone and telegraph operators
    3-80 Telephone and telegraph operators

3-9 Clerical and related workers not elsewhere classified
    3-91 Stock clerks
    3-92 Material and production planning clerks
    3-93 Correspondence and reporting clerks
    3-94 Receptionists and travel agency clerks
    3-95 Library and filing clerks
    3-99 Clerks not elsewhere classified

MAJOR GROUP 4: SALES WORKERS

4-0 Managers (wholesale and retail trade)
    4-00 Managers (wholesale and retail trade)

4-1 Working proprietors (wholesale and retail trade)
    4-10 Working proprietors (wholesale and retail trade)

4-2 Sales supervisors and buyers
    4-21 Sales supervisors
    4-22 Buyers

4-3 Technical salesmen, commercial travellers and manufacturers' agents
    4-31 Technical salesmen and service advisers
    4-32 Commercial travellers and manufacturers' agents

4-4 Insurance, real estate, securities and business services salesmen and auctioneers
    4-41 Insurance, real estate and securities salesmen
    4-42 Business services salesmen
    4-43 Auctioneers

4-5 Salesmen, shop assistants and related workers
    4-51 Salesmen, shop assistants and demonstrators
    4-52 Street vendors, canvassers and newsvendors

4-9 Sales workers not elsewhere classified
    4-90 Sales workers not elsewhere classified

Major Group 5: Service Workers

5-0 Managers (catering and lodging services)
    5-00 Managers (catering and lodging services)

5-1 Working proprietors (catering and lodging services)
    5-10 Working proprietors (catering and lodging services)

5-2 Housekeeping and related service supervisors
    5-20 Housekeeping and related service supervisors

5-3 Cooks, waiters, bartenders and related workers
    5-31 Cooks
    5-32 Waiters, bartenders and related workers

5-4 Maids and related housekeeping service workers not elsewhere classified
    5-40 Maids and related housekeeping service workers not elsewhere classified

5-5 Building caretakers, charworkers, cleaners and related workers
    5-51 Building caretakers
    5-52 Charworkers, cleaners and related workers

5-6 Launderers, dry-cleaners and pressers
    5-60 Launderers, dry-cleaners and pressers

5-7 Hairdressers, barbers, beauticians and related workers
    5-70 Hairdressers, barbers, beauticians and related workers

5-8 Protective service workers
    5-81 Fire-fighters
    5-82 Policemen and detectives
    5-89 Protective service workers not elsewhere classified

5-9 Service workers not elsewhere classified
    5-91 Guides
    5-92 Undertakers and embalmers
    5-99 Other service workers

Major Group 6: Agricultural, Animal Husbandry and Forestry Workers, Fishermen and Hunters

6-0 Farm managers and supervisors
    6-00 Farm managers and supervisors

6-1 Farmers
  6-11 General farmers
  6-12 Specialised farmers

6-2 Agricultural and animal husbandry workers
  6-21 General farm workers
  6-22 Field crop and vegetable growing workers
  6-23 Orchard, vineyard and related tree and shrub crop workers
  6-24 Livestock workers
  6-25 Dairy farm workers
  6-26 Poultry farm workers
  6-27 Nursery workers and gardeners
  6-28 Farm machinery operators
  6-29 Agricultural and animal husbandry workers not elsewhere classified

6-3 Forestry workers
  6-31 Loggers
  6-32 Forestry workers (except loggers)

6-4 Fishermen, hunters and related workers
  6-41 Fishermen
  6-49 Fishermen, hunters and related workers not elsewhere classified

MAJOR GROUP 7/8/9: PRODUCTION AND RELATED WORKERS, TRANSPORT
EQUIPMENT OPERATORS AND LABOURERS

7-0 Production supervisors and general foremen
  7-00 Production supervisors and general foremen

7-1 Miners, quarrymen, well drillers and related workers
  7-11 Miners and quarrymen
  7-12 Mineral and stone treaters
  7-13 Well drillers, borers and related workers

7-2 Metal processers
  7-21 Metal smelting, converting and refining furnacemen
  7-22 Metal rolling mill workers
  7-23 Metal melters and reheaters
  7-24 Metal casters
  7-25 Metal moulders and coremakers
  7-26 Metal annealers, temperers and case hardeners
  7-27 Metal drawers and extruders
  7-28 Metal platers and coaters
  7-29 Metal processers not elsewhere classified

7-3 Wood preparation workers and paper makers
  7-31 Wood treaters
  7-32 Sawyers, plywood makers and related wood processing workers
  7-33 Paper pulp preparers
  7-34 Paper makers

7-4 Chemical processers and related workers
  7-41 Crushers, grinders and mixers
  7-42 Cookers, roasters and related heat treaters
  7-43 Filter and separator operators

7-44   Still and reactor operators
7-45   Petroleum refining workers
7-49   Chemical processers and related workers not elsewhere classified

7-5   Spinners, weavers, knitters, dyers and related workers

7-51   Fibre preparers
7-52   Spinners and winders
7-53   Weaving and knitting machine setters and pattern-card preparers
7-54   Weavers and related workers
7-55   Knitters
7-56   Bleachers, dyers and textile product finishers
7-59   Spinners, weavers, knitters, dyers and related workers not elsewhere classified

7-6   Tanners, fellmongers and pelt dressers

7-61   Tanners and fellmongers
7-62   Pelt dressers

7-7   Food and beverage processers

7-71   Grain millers and related workers
7-72   Sugar processers and refiners
7-73   Butchers and meat preparers
7-74   Food preservers
7-75   Dairy product processers
7-76   Bakers, pastrycooks and confectionery makers
7-77   Tea, coffee and cocoa preparers
7-78   Brewers, wine and beverage makers
7-79   Food and beverage processers not elsewhere classified

7-8   Tobacco preparers and tobacco product makers

7-81   Tobacco preparers
7-82   Cigar makers
7-83   Cigarette makers
7-89   Tobacco preparers and tobacco product makers not elsewhere classified

7-9   Tailors, dressmakers, sewers, upholsterers and related workers

7-91   Tailors and dressmakers
7-92   Fur tailors
7-93   Milliners and hatmakers
7-94   Patternmakers and cutters
7-95   Sewers and embroiderers
7-96   Upholsterers and related workers
7-99   Tailors, dressmakers, sewers, upholsterers and related workers not elsewhere classified

8-0   Shoemakers and leather goods makers

8-01   Shoemakers and shoe repairers
8-02   Shoe cutters, lasters, sewers and related workers
8-03   Leather goods makers

8-1   Cabinetmakers and related wood workers

8-11   Cabinetmakers
8-12   Woodworking-machine operators
8-19   Cabinetmakers and related wood workers not elsewhere classified

8-2   Stone cutters and carvers

8-20   Stone cutters and carvers

8-3　Blacksmiths, toolmakers and machine tool operators
　　8-31　Blacksmiths, hammersmiths and forging-press operators
　　8-32　Toolmakers, metal pattern makers and metal markers
　　8-33　Machine tool setter-operators
　　8-34　Machine tool operators
　　8-35　Metal grinders, polishers and tool sharpeners
　　8-39　Blacksmiths, toolmakers and machine tool operators not elsewhere classified

8-4　Machinery fitters, machine assemblers and precision instrument makers (except electrical)
　　8-41　Machinery fitters and machine assemblers
　　8-42　Watch, clock and precision instrument makers
　　8-43　Motor vehicle mechanics
　　8-44　Aircraft engine mechanics
　　8-49　Machinery fitters, machine assemblers and precision instrument makers (except electrical) not elsewhere classified

8-5　Electrical fitters and related electrical and electronics workers
　　8-51　Electrical fitters
　　8-52　Electronics fitters
　　8-53　Electrical and electronic equipment assemblers
　　8-54　Radio and television repairmen
　　8-55　Electrical wiremen
　　8-56　Telephone and telegraph installers
　　8-57　Electric linemen and cable jointers
　　8-59　Electrical fitters and related electrical and electronics workers not elsewhere classified

8-6　Broadcasting station and sound equipment operators and cinema projectionists
　　8-61　Broadcasting station operators
　　8-62　Sound equipment operators and cinema projectionists

8-7　Plumbers, welders, sheet metal and structural metal preparers and erectors
　　8-71　Plumbers and pipe fitters
　　8-72　Welders and flame cutters
　　8-73　Sheet metal workers
　　8-74　Structural metal preparers and erectors

8-8　Jewellery and precious metal workers
　　8-80　Jewellery and precious metal workers

8-9　Glass formers, potters and related workers

　　8-91　Glass formers, cutters, grinders and finishers
　　8-92　Potters and related clay and abrasive formers
　　8-93　Glass and ceramics kilnmen
　　8-94　Glass engravers and etchers
　　8-95　Glass and ceramics painters and decorators
　　8-99　Glass formers, potters and related workers not elsewhere classified

9-0　Rubber and plastics product makers
　　9-01　Rubber and plastics product makers (except tyre makers and tyre vulcanisers)
　　9-02　Tyre makers and vulcanisers

9-1   Paper-and-paperboard products makers
     9-10   Paper-and-paperboard products makers

9-2   Printers and related workers
     9-21   Compositors and typesetters
     9-22   Printing pressmen
     9-23   Stereotypers and electrotypers
     9-24   Printing engravers (except photo-engravers)
     9-25   Photo-engravers
     9-26   Bookbinders and related workers
     9-27   Photographic darkroom workers
     9-29   Printers and related workers not elsewhere classified

9-3   Painters
     9-31   Painters, construction
     9-39   Painters not elsewhere classified

9-4   Production and related workers not elsewhere classified
     9-41   Musical instrument makers and tuners
     9-42   Basketry weavers and brush makers
     9-43   Non-metallic mineral product makers
     9-49   Other production and related workers

9-5   Bricklayers, carpenters and other construction workers
     9-51   Bricklayers, stonemasons and tile setters
     9-52   Reinforced-concreters, cement finishers and terrazzo workers
     9-53   Roofers
     9-54   Carpenters, joiners and parquetry workers
     9-55   Plasterers
     9-56   Insulators
     9-57   Glaziers
     9-59   Construction workers not elsewhere classified

9-6   Stationary engines and related equipment operators
     9-61   Power generating machinery operators
     9-69   Stationary engine and related equipment operators not elsewhere classified

9-7   Material-handling and related equipment operators, dockers and freight handlers
     9-71   Dockers and freight handlers
     9-72   Riggers and cable splicers
     9-73   Crane and hoist operators
     9-74   Earth-moving and related machinery operators
     9-79   Material-handling equipment operators not elsewhere classified

9-8   Transport equipment operators
     9-81   Ships' deck ratings, barge crews and boatmen
     9-82   Ships' engine room ratings
     9-83   Railway engine drivers and firemen
     9-84   Railway brakemen, signalmen and shunters
     9-85   Motor vehicle drivers
     9-86   Animal and animal-drawn vehicle drivers
     9-89   Transport equipment operators not elsewhere classified

9-9   Labourers not elsewhere classified
  9-99   Labourers not elsewhere classified

MAJOR GROUP X: WORKERS NOT CLASSIFIABLE BY OCCUPATION

X-1   New workers seeking employment

X-10   New workers seeking employment

X-2   Workers reporting occupations unidentifiable or inadequately described

X-20   Workers reporting occupations unidentifiable or inadequately described

X-3   Workers not reporting any occupation

X-30   Workers not reporting any occupation

ARMED FORCES: MEMBERS OF THE ARMED FORCES

**E.   International classification according to status (as employer, employee, etc.):
Definitions of status adopted by the Statistical Commission of the United Nations
(Fourteenth Session, October 1966)**

Status (as employer, employee, etc.) refers to the status of an economically active individual with respect to his employment, that is, whether he is (or was, if unemployed) an employer, own-account worker, employee, unpaid family worker, or a member of a producers' co-operative, as defined below:

(a) Employer: a person who operates his or her own economic enterprise or engages independently in a profession or trade, and hires one or more employees. Some countries may wish to distinguish among employers according to the number of persons they employ.

(b) Own-account worker: a person who operates his or her own economic enterprise or engages independently in a profession or trade, and hires no employees.

(c) Employee: a person who works for a public or private employer and receives remuneration in wages, salary, commission, tips, piece-rates or pay in kind.

(d) Unpaid family worker: a person who works a specified minimum amount of time (at least one-third of normal working hours), without pay, in an economic enterprise operated by a related person living in the same household. If there are a significant number of unpaid family workers in enterprises of which the operators are members of a producers' co-operative who are classified in category *(e)*, these unpaid family workers should be classified in a separate sub-group.

(e) Member of producers' co-operative: a person who is an active member of a producers' co-operative, regardless of the industry in which it is established. Where this group is not numerically important, it may be excluded from the classification and members of producers' co-operatives should be classified to other headings, as appropriate.

(f) Persons not classifiable by status: experienced workers with status unknown or inadequately described and unemployed persons not previously employed.

LABOUR FORCE, EMPLOYMENT, UNEMPLOYMENT AND UNDEREMPLOYMENT

2

LABOUR FORCE, EMPLOYMENT AND UNEMPLOYMENT

The question of unemployment statistics was included in the agenda of the Second International Conference of Labour Statisticians (1925), to which a study on methods prepared by the ILO had been submitted [1]. The Conference adopted recommendations relating to unemployment statistics based on unemployment insurance or on the data of employment offices or on population censuses or, lastly, on special inquiries relating to the whole population or to a sample of the population [2].

Population censuses provide a basic source of data on employment and unemployment. Until the Second World War it was primarily from these censuses that statistics of the "economically active population" depended. In 1938 the Committee of Statistical Experts of the League of Nations drew up proposals for improving international comparability of census data on the economically active population [3], including a definition of that population (see "Texts", item A). In the ensuing years a considerable expansion in statistics of employment took place in many countries. The technique of sample surveys pointed the way to a more comprehensive approach towards data on employment and unemployment. In addition, there appeared the concept of "labour force".

In 1947 the Sixth International Conference of Labour Statisticians took up anew the question of labour force, employment and unemployment statistics on the basis of a study relating to methods that had been prepared by the ILO [4]. In the resolution that it adopted on that question, the Conference defined employment, unemployment and labour force mainly on the basis of the activity of each individual during a specified period; this was a departure from the "gainful worker" concept (most commonly used in the past), according to which the classification of a person as employed or unemployed was not related as strictly to activity during any specified time period. Furthermore, the Conference urged that a new examination of the international recommendations be made as soon as advances in methods or experience gained seemed to make such further consideration desirable [5].

This was done in 1954 by the Eighth International Conference of Labour Statisticians, for which a report on employment and unemployment statistics had been prepared by the Office [6, 7]. That Conference adopted a resolution (see "Texts", item B) superseding the one adopted by the Sixth Conference in which it gave detailed definitions for the labour force, employment and unemployment and which contained recommendations on the scope and nature of the statistics that should be made available by each country in these fields.

The Statistical Commission of the United Nations, for its part, included some recommendations relating to the economically active population (see "Texts", item C) in the principles and recommendations relating to the population censuses of 1970 which it adopted in 1966 [8].

UNDEREMPLOYMENT

The international recommendations based on traditional methods of measuring employment and unemployment are not adequate to cope with the problem of underemployment, particularly in the developing countries, where they lose a great deal of their meaning. The Sixth International Conference of Labour Statisticians in 1947, the United Nations Committee of Experts on the International Definition and Measurement of Standards and Levels of Living in 1953 and the Eighth International Conference of Labour Statisticians in 1954 all urged the ILO to study the problems involved in the measurement of underemployment.

The Office prepared a report on the subject for the consideration of the Ninth International Conference of Labour Statisticians in 1957 [9]. The Conference adopted a resolution proposing certain preliminary steps towards the establishment of international standards, defining visible and invisible underemployment and laying down certain rules for the measurement of visible underemployment [10]. In addition, it urged the development of methods of research, especially in the developing countries, with a view to analysing the various aspects of invisible underemployment.

The Meeting of Experts on the Measurement of Underemployment, held in 1963 under the auspices of the ILO, re-examined the concepts, definitions and methods of collection and analysis of the data. On the basis of its recommendations [11], the Office prepared a new report [12] for the Eleventh International Conference of Labour Statisticians (1966), which was called upon to amend the resolution of 1957 in the light of national and international experience and to draw up new guidelines [13].

The Eleventh Conference adopted a resolution superseding the resolution of 1957 (see "Texts", item D). It contains detailed definitions of visible underemployment and of invisible underemployment (disguised underemployment, potential underemployment) and brings out the importance of analysing the various types of underemployment. It also touches on the question of the study of under-utilisation of manpower.

References

[1] ILO: *Methods of statistics of unemployment*, Studies and reports, Series N, No. 7 (Geneva, 1925).

[2] — *The Second International Conference of Labour Statisticians*, Studies and reports, Series N, No. 8 (Geneva, 1925), pp. 48-67.

[3] League of Nations: *Statistics of the Gainfully Occupied Population. Definitions and Classifications Recommended by the Committee of Statistical Experts* (1938, II. A. 12), Studies and reports on statistical methods, No. 1 (Geneva, 1938).

[4] ILO: *Employment, unemployment and labour force statistics*, Studies and reports, New series, No. 7, Part 1 (Geneva, 1948).

[5] — *The Sixth International Conference of Labour Statisticians*, Studies and reports, New series, No. 7, Part 4 (Geneva, 1948), pp. 9-25 and 52-60.

[6] — *Employment and unemployment statistics*, Eighth International Conference of Labour Statisticians, Report IV (Geneva, 1954; mimeographed).

[7] — *The Eighth International Conference of Labour Statisticians, 1954* (Geneva, 1955; mimeographed), pp. 22-29 and 42-49.

[8] United Nations: *Principles and Recommendations for the 1970 Population Censuses*, Statistical papers, Series M, No. 44 (New York, 1967), paras. 290-294.

[9] ILO: *Measurement of underemployment*, Ninth International Conference of Labour Statisticians, Report IV (Geneva, 1957; mimeographed).

[10] — *Ninth International Conference of Labour Statisticians, 1957* (Geneva; mimeographed), pp. 34-37 and 82-86.

[11] — *Report of the meeting of experts on measurement of underemployment* (Geneva, doc. MEMU/D.4, 1963; mimeographed).

[12] — *Measurement of underemployment: concepts and methods*, Eleventh International Conference of Labour Statisticians, Report IV (Geneva, 1966; mimeographed).

[13] — *The Eleventh International Conference of Labour Statisticians, 1966* (Geneva, 1967; mimeographed), pp. 24-29 and 56-59.

Texts

A. Definition of the gainfully occupied population as recommended by the Committee of Statistical Experts of the League of Nations in 1938

For the purpose of international classification, any occupation for which the person engaged therein is remunerated, directly or indirectly, in cash or in kind—i.e. any principal remunerated occupation or any secondary occupation which is the sole remunerated occupation of the person concerned—is to be considered as a gainful occupation. Housework done by members of a family in their own homes is not included in that description, but work done by members of a family in helping the head of the family in his occupation is so included, even though only indirectly remunerated. The occupation of persons working in labour camps or other similar institutions or on unemployment relief projects is to be considered as a gainful occupation.

The particulars given should be based, generally speaking, on the occupation at the moment of the census. A person who has recently exercised a gainful occupation is to be considered as still engaged in that occupation even though, by reason of sickness, injury, vacation or inability to obtain work, he may, at the time of the census, be temporarily not working.

Young persons of working age and not at school, who have never actually exercised a gainful occupation, are not to be treated as part of the gainfully occupied population, even though they may be seeking work and consequently included in statistics of unemployment. It is, however, desirable that censuses should be so taken that the number of young persons in this situation can be ascertained.

B. Resolution concerning statistics of the labour force, employment and unemployment adopted by the Eighth International Conference of Labour Statisticians (November-December 1954)

The Eighth International Conference of Labour Statisticians,

. . . .

Recognising the usefulness of such standards in the provision of technical assistance to countries with less well developed statistics, and in the provision of guidance to all countries in efforts to obtain international comparability,

Adopts, this third day of December 1954, the following resolution in substitution for Resolution I of the Sixth Conference:

GENERAL OBJECTIVES

1. Every country should aim to develop a comprehensive system of statistics of the labour force, employment and unemployment, in order to provide an adequate statistical basis for the analysis of economic and social problems of the labour force, of employment and unemployment, and, in particular, for the formulation and application of policies designed to promote economic development.

2. These statistics should be developed in accordance with the specific needs of each country in the light of its social and economic structure and, in so far as possible, in accordance with international standards in order to promote comparability among countries.

3. All member countries should make every effort to supply statistics to the International Labour Office on the basis of these standards.

DEFINITIONS

Definition of labour force

4. The civilian labour force consists of all civilians who fulfil the requirements for inclusion among the employed or the unemployed, as defined in paragraphs 6 and 7 below.

5. The total labour force is the sum of the civilian labour force and the armed forces.

Definition of employment

6. (1) Persons in employment consist of all persons above a specified age in the following categories:

(a) at work; persons who performed some work for pay or profit during a specified brief period, either one week or one day;

(b) with a job but not at work; persons who, having already worked in their present job, were temporarily absent during the specified period because of illness or injury, industrial dispute, vacation or other leave of absence, absence without leave, or temporary disorganisation of work due to such reasons as bad weather or mechanical breakdown.

(2) Employers and workers on own account should be included among the employed and may be classified as "at work" or "not at work" on the same basis as other employed persons.

(3) Unpaid family workers currently assisting in the operation of a business or farm are considered as employed if they worked for at least one-third of the normal working time during the specified period.

(4) The following categories of persons are not considered as employed:

(a) workers who during the specified period were on temporary or indefinite lay-off without pay;

(b) persons without jobs or businesses or farms who had arranged to start a new job or business or farm at a date subsequent to the period of reference;

(c) unpaid members of the family who worked for less than one-third of the normal working time during the specified period in a family business or farm.

Definition of unemployment

7. (1) Persons in unemployment consist of all persons above a specified age who, on the specified day or for a specified week, were in the following categories:

(a) workers available for employment whose contract of employment had been terminated or temporarily suspended and who were without a job and seeking work for pay or profit;

(b) persons who were available for work (except for minor illness) during the specified period and were seeking work for pay or profit, who were never previously employed or whose most recent status was other than that of employee (i.e. former employers, etc.), or who had been in retirement;

(c) persons without a job and currently available for work who had made arrangements to start a new job at a date subsequent to the specified period;

(d) persons on temporary or indefinite lay-off without pay.

(2) The following categories of persons are not considered to be unemployed:

(a) persons intending to establish their own business or farm, but who had not yet arranged to do so, who were not seeking work for pay or profit;

(b) former unpaid family workers not at work and not seeking work for pay or profit.

CLASSIFICATIONS

8. Persons in the labour force should be classified in occupational groups which are convertible into the International Standard Classification of Occupations as adopted by the Seventh International Conference of Labour Statisticians. When a more detailed classification has been adopted by a future International Conference of Labour Statisticians it should be used as the revised standard for the classification of persons in the labour force.

9. Classification of persons in the labour force, the employed and the unemployed (the latter on the basis of their last activity) according to branch of economic activity should adhere to or be convertible into the International Standard Industrial Classification of All Economic Activities.

10. Persons in the labour force, the employed and the unemployed (the latter on the basis of their last activity) when classified by status (as employer, employee, etc.), should be distributed among the following groups, pending the possible modification of these groups by the United Nations or specialised agencies on the basis of the results of the 1950 censuses:

(1) employees;

(2) employers;

(3) persons who work on their own account without employees;

(4) unpaid family workers.

11. (1) The classification used in presenting statistics of unemployment according to duration should permit data to be derived for the following intervals: less than one week, one week or more but less than one month, one month or more but less than three months, three months or more but less than six months, six months or more.

(2) For the purpose of statistics on duration of unemployment, duration means the period from the commencement of the current unemployment status up to the date of the count.

Scope and Nature of Statistics

12. The statistics of the labour force, employment and unemployment developed by each country should cover—

(1) all branches of economic activity;

(2) all persons, employed and unemployed;

(3) all status groups (employers, employees, etc.).

13. Such statistics should provide—

(1) comprehensive basic data in the fullest possible detail at convenient intervals (hereinafter referred to as "benchmark data"); and

(2) series, not necessarily in the same detail, to show current changes.

Benchmark data

14. A population census should be taken at least every ten years and should provide detailed statistics of employment, unemployment and the labour force, including data for each sex, classified by—

(1) status (as employer, employee, etc.);

(2) branch of economic activity;

(3) occupational group;

(4) age group;

(5) marital status;

(6) region.

15. Censuses of establishments engaged in agriculture, mining and manufacturing, and, if practicable, in other divisions of economic activity, should be taken in every country at least every ten years and should provide detailed basic statistics of employment, including data for each sex, classified by—

(1) status (as employer, employee, etc.);

(2) branch of economic activity;

(3) region;

(4) size of establishment (according to number employed);

(5) form of ownership of establishment (private, public, co-operative, etc.).

Labour force, employment, unemployment and underemployment

Labour force data

16. Every country should prepare estimates of the civilian labour force classified by sex and age at least once a year.

Employment data

17. The principal series relied upon to show current changes in employment should yield at least the following information:

(1) once each year, the number of employed persons of each sex, classified by—

   (a) age;

   (b) status (as employer, employee, etc.);

   (c) employment in agriculture and non-agricultural industries;

(2) once each quarter, the number of employees (wage earners and salaried employees) in non-agricultural industries, with separate data for each industry in which as much as 5 per cent of the country's total employment is found;

(3) separate series should be made available periodically for—

   (a) persons included among the employed in a specified period who were not at work, classified by cause of absence from work;

   (b) employed persons classified according to the number of hours worked per week;

(4) where seasonal changes in agricultural employment are substantial, estimates of agricultural employment, based on special studies, should be made more frequently than once a year in order to measure the seasonal movement;

(5) any country which has not established a series on the general level of employment should lay the foundations for such a series by commencing to collect data relating to persons of each sex employed in establishments, beginning with manufacturing industry and extending the collection to other branches of economic activity as resources and facilities become available.

Unemployment data

18. Series showing the total numbers unemployed, analysed by sex, should be prepared at least quarterly.

19. The data used as a basis of unemployment statistics should be analysed at least twice a year to show the numbers of unemployed persons of each sex according to—

(1) branch of economic activity in which last employed;

(2) occupational group;

(3) region;

(4) age group;

(5) duration of unemployment.

20. The number of unemployed persons classified by age and sex, as well as by duration of unemployment, should be provided, periodically at least, for those regions in which unemployment is particularly severe.

21. The data used as a basis of unemployment statistics should be analysed at least once a year to show the numbers of unemployed persons of each sex who—

(1) were temporarily laid off (laid off with instructions to return to work within 30 days);

(2) had found paid employment but had not yet started to work;

(3) were on indefinite lay-off or had no job attachment.

22. Statistics on unemployment do not have the same significance in industrially less developed countries as in other countries, and should not have the same priority in the national statistical programme; however, a country wishing to start collecting data on this question might commence with data relating to the principal urban centres, collected by means of labour force sample surveys or as part of more general sample surveys.

PUBLICATION

23. (1) Statistics of employment, unemployment and the labour force should be issued promptly and made widely available. Final or provisional key totals in current series should be released for publication with the least possible delay and, wherever practicable, within one month of the date to which they refer.

(2) Every publication of statistical data relating to employment, unemployment or the labour force, whether recurring or single-time, should clearly indicate the nature of the data and make reference to any detailed technical descriptions available.

C. Definitions adopted by the Statistical Commission of the United Nations concerning the economically active population and the type of activity (Fourteenth Session, October 1966)

Economically active population comprises all persons of either sex who furnish the supply of labour for the production of economic goods and services during the time-reference period chosen for the investigation. It includes both persons in the civilian labour force and those serving in the armed forces. In compilations of the data, a separate category of "members of the armed forces" may be maintained, so that the category can be deducted from the total labour force whenever desirable. The civilian labour force comprises both persons employed and those unemployed during the time-reference period.

. . . .

Type of activity is the relationship of each person to current economic activity. Information should be collected for each person at or above the minimum age for which economic characteristics are to be tabulated as to whether or not the person is economically active.

Particular attention should be given to groups which may be especially difficult to classify, such as female unpaid family workers in agriculture, young persons seeking work for the first time, and persons receiving pensions consequent upon retirement from one job who are, at the same time, working at another job. . . .

The minimum age-limit adopted for the census questions on economic activity should be set in accordance with the conditions in each country, but never higher than 15 years. Those countries which have a large proportion of their labour force engaged in agriculture, a type of activity in which, normally, many children participate, will need to select a lower minimum age than highly industrialised countries, where employment of young children is rare. In order to permit international comparisons of data on the economically active population, however, any tabulations of economic characteristics not cross-classified by detailed age should at least distinguish between persons under 15 years of age and those 15 years of age and over.

The adoption of a specific time reference for census data on economic characteristics is fundamental to the concept of the economically active population. It is recommended that the time-reference period should be not longer than one week. Where it is considered that classification on the basis of current activity over this brief time period does not reflect year-round activities, particularly where there is a highly seasonal pattern of employment and regular periodic sample surveys are not held during the year, supplementary information on "usual" economic characteristics over a longer period may also be collected. Such supplementary information might also prove useful in enabling comparisons to be made between the results obtained when the brief time-reference period is used and when a longer period is employed, in order to ascertain the effect of different time references.

D. Resolution concerning measurement and analysis of underemployment and under-utilisation of manpower adopted by the Eleventh International Conference of Labour Statisticians (October 1966)

The Eleventh International Conference of Labour Statisticians,

. . . .

Believing that revised guidelines for the further development of underemployment measurement and analysis would be useful, especially in developing countries,

Adopts, this twenty-sixth day of October 1966, the following resolution in substitution of Resolution III of the Ninth International Conference of Labour Statisticians:

GENERAL OBJECTIVES

1. The primary object of measurement and analysis of underemployment and other aspects of the under-utilisation of manpower is to contribute towards making and appraising short-term and long-term policies and measures, and in particular manpower planning and projections, designed to promote "full, productive and freely chosen" employment as specified in the Convention and Recommendation (No. 122) concerning employment policy adopted by the International Labour Conference in 1964.

2. Special attention might be paid to underemployment in economic sectors, in regions and for worker categories particularly affected by underemployment and which constitute acute problems in national conditions. Pertinent examples are peasant farming, especially in developing countries, other smaller establishments, economically lagging regions, declining industries, e.g., coal mining in industrialised countries, seasonal work, such as in agriculture or construction, and worker categories particularly vulnerable to discrimination in employment on grounds of sex, age, nationality, race, etc.

3. In developing countries, preliminary information on underemployment could be obtained as a part of household surveys. Resurveys or detailed surveys of underemployment would be necessary when it is desired to make or appraise short-term or long-term programmes for remedying structural underemployment.

UNDEREMPLOYMENT

Concepts of underemployment

4. Underemployment exists when a person's employment is inadequate, in relation to specified norms or alternative employment, account being taken of his occupational skill (training and working experience). Two principal forms of underemployment may be distinguished: visible and invisible.

5. (1) Visible underemployment is primarily a statistical concept directly measurable by labour force and other surveys, reflecting an insufficiency in the volume of employment. It occurs when a person is in employment of less than normal duration and is seeking, or would accept, additional work.

(2) Invisible underemployment is primarily an analytical concept reflecting a misallocation of labour resources or a fundamental imbalance as between labour and other factors of production. Characteristic symptoms might be low income, under-utilisation of skill, low productivity. Analytical studies of invisible underemployment should be directed to the examination and analysis of a wide variety of data, including income and skill levels (disguised underemployment) and productivity measures (potential underemployment) to which some further reference is made below.

Elements and methods of measurement and analysis of visible underemployment

6. Two major elements of the measurement and analytical estimation of visible underemployment may be distinguished:

(a) the number of underemployed persons;

(b) the quantity of underemployment (in terms of man-years, man-days and man-hours, etc.).

7. (1) For the purpose of identifying persons in visible underemployment as well as for other purposes, such as providing estimates of labour input, persons in employment should be classified according to duration of work. For different countries, and for different purposes, "duration of work" may be measured in terms of hours or days per week, days per month, days or weeks per year and so on. Where the period is one week, from the point of view of international comparisons, it would be useful if, in addition to whatever categories are used for the country's own analysis, the results could be made convertible to the following categories:

(a) according to hours of work per week: less than 15, 15-34, 35-39, 40-47, 48 or more;

(b) according to days of work per week: less than 2, 2-4, 5 or more.

(2) For purposes of identifying and classifying persons in visible underemployment, all persons in employment of less than normal duration for economic reasons should be classified according to pertinent characteristics such as sex, age group, branch of activity, status (as employer, employee, etc.), duration of work and, where possible, income. Classification by extra time available for work (not exceeding the normal duration), while also useful, requires to be interpreted with caution since it involves subjective elements whose influence is generally difficult to control in survey procedures.

(3) The seasonal and chronic components of visible underemployment should be distinguished where feasible, especially in agriculture.

8. Data on visibly underemployed persons may be obtained within the framework of labour force and other surveys.[1] If the survey provides for observation of labour force characteristics on a current basis over a full year, comprehensive and reliable data on seasonal changes in employment may be obtained. As a minimum the data should be based on current observation at two points of time within a 12-month period, preferably corresponding to seasonal peak and slack.

9. The quantity of visible underemployment, expressed in terms of labour units in man-years, man-days or man-hours, etc., can be estimated by analysis of data on the distribution of visibly underemployed persons by the duration of work or the duration of extra time available for work. In practice, a variery of such estimates may be derived depending on the assumptions made and the analytical methods followed.

---

[1] In this resolution, the term "labour force survey" also covers general-purpose household surveys within the framework of which information on the economic activity of the population is collected.

Elements and methods of measurement and analysis of invisible underemployment

Disguised underemployment

10. (1) For the purposes of analysing disguised underemployment, information on income is essential. In developing countries satisfactory estimates of data on income can generally be obtained by labour force sample surveys only in regard to paid employees; for other worker categories elaborate family budget surveys may supply usable data on broad income groups. In developed countries and, in some cases, in developing countries as well, satisfactory data on earnings may be available from labour force sample surveys and from other sources such as tax returns.

(2) Methodology for the analysis of disguised underemployment according to the skill under-utilisation criterion still remains to be developed. Experimental surveys and studies, particularly in regard to limited sectors or specific worker categories concerned, should be undertaken for the purpose.

Potential underemployment

11. (1) Potential underemployment, an aspect of underemployment which may be studied by the criterion of low labour productivity, may be considered to exist when a person is employed in an establishment or economic unit whose productivity is abnormally low.

(2) The primary focus of interest in the productivity approach to underemployment is in the dynamic assessment of the relationship between labour availability and needs over time as productivity rises in the process of economic development and in sectoral and regional productivity comparisons.

(3) The potentially underemployed cannot be directly identified but where detailed data on the labour force and production are available analysis based on these data may provide broad indicators of the number and characteristics of persons potentially underemployed and the amount of such underemployment.

(4) In various sectors of the economy, in particular in agriculture, estimation of "labour surplus" or "labour force reserves" can be obtained by comparing labour units available and labour units actually utilised or required under various assumptions regarding productivity.

Further action

12. Countries undertaking inquiries and analyses of different forms of invisible underemployment, especially in relation to agriculture in developing countries, are urged to report their experience to the International Labour Office in order that these methods of study may be considered by a future International Conference of Labour Statisticians.

Statistical and analytical development

13. Where appropriate, underemployment statistics should be consistent with, and in so far as possible be integrated into, the system of labour force, employment and unemployment statistics set forth in Resolution I adopted by the Eighth International Conference of Labour Statisticians.[1]

14. Consideration should be given to initiating or strengthening a system of labour force sample surveys in developing countries where appropriate. Such a system may be needed as an integral part of a comprehensive framework of labour force data required, among other things, for analysing underemployment. At the same time it can

---

[1] See above, Text B.

provide direct measurement of major elements of underemployment and especially visible underemployment.

15. General-purpose surveys of wide scope, such as labour force sample surveys, should be supplemented by an adequate programme of limited but intensive special surveys aimed at studying underemployment in depth or providing regional or local data. In addition, it is recommended that countries pursue methodological studies with the aim of reducing the uncertainties inherent in sample surveys and develop research on appropriate analytical methods leading to results as significant as possible.

16. For measuring and analysing varied aspects of underemployment, existing statistical and technical data should be fully drawn upon. Major pertinent statistical sources include, besides labour force sample surveys, family budget surveys, population censuses, agricultural and industrial censuses, periodic establishment reports, records of placement services and national accounts. Sources of technical data include special surveys and records primarily of a non-statistical nature, such as farm management and time utilisation surveys and records of agricultural extension programmes.

17. Where appropriate, countries should endeavour to develop adequate programmes of statistical and analytical studies of underemployment focused on current and urgent problems, especially the requirements of development planning bodies.

UNDER-UTILISATION OF MANPOWER

18. In addition to those persons who are in the current labour force but whose contribution to the incomes of their families and to the national product is limited by unemployment or underemployment, there are in many countries persons who are not in the labour force but who would enter it under certain circumstances. Such persons may not be actively seeking work, for example, because no suitable work is available for them; or they may be discouraged because they are victims of prejudice or are refugees; or they may suffer from physical or mental handicaps which could be overcome by means of training or other remedial action. Although it is important for every country to know the extent to which its manpower resources are under-utilised, satisfactory methods of measurement have not yet been developed and tested. Countries undertaking studies of under-utilisation of manpower are urged to report their experience to the Internationl Labour Office, in order that effective methods of study may be considered by a future International Conference of Labour Statisticians.

WAGES, HOURS OF WORK, LABOUR COST AND EMPLOYEE INCOME 3

The various subjects to which the title of this chapter refers are closely inter-connected and have often been considered together by the conferences that have been concerned with the standardisation of the corresponding statistics. It is, for that matter, an integrated system of statistics in this field which the Twelfth International Conference of Labour Statisticians (1973) recommended.

WAGES AND HOURS OF WORK

The subject of statistics of wages and hours of work was one of the topics on the agenda of the First International Conference of Labour Statisticians in 1923, for which the ILO prepared a report dealing with statistical methods [1]. The Conference adopted a resolution (see "Texts", item A) covering the types of statistics to be established (rates of pay, actual earnings, normal hours of work and actual hours of work) and on the principles to be followed in that regard. It also recommended that index numbers should be computed to show the general course of changes in nominal wage rates and in actual earnings [2].

Two conferences of statisticians convened by the Social Science Research Council of the United States, which were held in 1929 and in 1930 at the ILO in Geneva, gave special attention to the question of index numbers of wages. In its conclusions (see "Texts", item B), the first of these conferences made recom-mendations on the establishment of wages indices for measuring: *(a)* changes in the general standard of living of the workers, *(b)* changes in the standard of living within the various industries or within the various groups of workers in each country, *(c)* changes in wages as an aid to forecasting economic condi-tions, *(d)* earnings per hour in respect of work of comparable character and efficiency, *(e)* labour cost per unit of production, and *(f)* changes in the pro-portion of the national income formed by wages. The second of these con-ferences engaged in a more detailed study of certain specific points relating to

the collection and organisation of the data, among others the differences between rates and earnings, the importance of the industries covered and the
problem of whether or not to include women's rates in a general index (see
"Texts", item C).

In 1931 the Fourth International Conference of Labour Statisticians adopted
a series of resolutions regarding the statistics of money wages to be established for purposes of the international comparison of real wages. It recommended
that the question of the availability of data on wages should be considered with
reference to the framing of an international Convention.

On the basis of a draft prepared by the Fifth International Conference of
Labour Statisticians (1937), the International Labour Conference adopted in
1938 at its 24th Session [3] the Convention (No. 63) concerning statistics of
wages and hours of work (see "Texts", item D). This Convention lays down
minimum standards for statistics of average earnings and hours actually worked
in the principal mining and manufacturing industries, including building and
construction (Part II) and statistics of time rates of wages and of normal hours
of work in the same industries (Part III), as well as statistics of wages and hours
of work in agriculture (Part IV). A ratifying country may exclude any one or
two of Parts II, III or IV from the scope of ratification, provided that it ratifies
either Part II or Part III. At 1 September 1975 the Convention had been ratified
in whole or in part by 32 countries.

The subject of statistics of wages was re-examined after the Second World
War in 1949 by the Seventh International Conference of Labour Statisticians,
which had before it an ILO report [4]. The Conference adopted a resolution on
methods to be used in obtaining statistics of earnings from payroll data (see
"Texts", item F). This Conference also studied the possibility of improving and
amplifying the statistics compiled in pursuance of the Convention of 1938 in
countries with a highly developed system of labour statistics. The resolution it
adopted on the subject (see "Texts", item E) repeats the text of the proposed
recommendation which had been submitted in 1938 by the Fifth International
Conference of Labour Statisticians to, but not considered by, the International
Labour Conference. The resolution urges that statistics of earnings and hours
of work shall be compiled in greater detail than provided for by the Convention,
as well as the regular compilation of statistics showing the aggregate amount
of wages and salaries paid annually in each of the principal industries; it also
recommends that statistics of wages by industries be published in terms of
the United Nations International Standard Industrial Classification of All
Economic Activities [5].

As for statistics of hours of work, the ILO convened in 1962 a Committee of
Experts which reviewed the whole question of the preparation of international
recommendations in that field, with particular reference to definitions, meth-

odology and tabulation. On the basis of that Committee's recommendations [6] and of information obtained from the countries compiling such statistics, the ILO prepared a report which was submitted to the Tenth International Conference of Labour Statisticians in 1962 [7]. In its resolution (see "Texts", item G), which deals with normal hours of work and with hours actually worked and which is applicable to wage earners and to salaried employees, the Conference specified the objectives to be aimed at, the definitions and the methods of collection of the data and of compilation and presentation of these statistics [8].

LABOUR COST

In view of the interest taken by the First European Regional Conference of the International Labour Organisation (1955) in the question of labour cost, the ILO carried out an inquiry into the cost of labour in European industry which showed the need for a comprehensive study of the problems involved in defining the various components of labour cost and in classifying the sums paid by employers to their staff.

In 1964 the ILO convened a Meeting of Experts for the purpose of defining the constituent elements of wages and of labour cost and of advising it on the preparation of statistical standards. The Meeting's conclusions [9] served as a basis for a report prepared by the Office for the Eleventh International Conference of Labour Statisticians (1966). The report dealt with the nature and purposes of labour cost statistics, the differences between labour cost and employee income, concepts and basic definitions, as well as the classification of data and the compilation of statistics [10]. The Conference adopted a resolution (see "Texts", item H) which laid down for the first time international standards in this field and which included in an annex an international standard classification of labour costs [11].

INTEGRATED SYSTEM OF WAGES STATISTICS

It appeared a few years ago that, if fuller and more reliable information on the various forms of remuneration of wage earners was to become available, it would be indispensable to revise and broaden the international standards that had been developed over the years with respect to wages and related statistics. Accordingly, the ILO convened in 1968 a Meeting of Experts to advise on the preparation of new international standards in that field. In its report [12] the Meeting proposed the establishment of an integrated system of wages and employee income statistics and made a number of recommendations on concepts and basic definitions and on the compilation of statistics. Its conclusions were widely disseminated and gave rise to comments on the part of 26 national statistical offices and six international or regional organisations.

The question was subsequently included in the agenda of the Twelfth International Conference of Labour Statisticians (1973). The Office's report [13] contained a detailed study of wages statistics which, it suggested, should be embodied in an integrated system covering both the agricultural and the non-agricultural sectors. It is a system of that kind which the Conference recommended in the resolution which it adopted on this question. Under that system the statistics of earnings, wage rates, hours of work, structure and distribution of wages, as well as labour cost, would be rearranged and brought together. The system provides for a programme of current statistics designed to meet short-term needs as well as a programme of less frequent statistics to meet long-term and standing requirements [14]. The Conference's resolution indicates the general objectives and scope of the system, concepts and definitions, as well as the characteristics and methods of compilation of wages statistics, including especially agricultural wages statistics (see "Texts", item I).

References

[1] ILO: *Methods of statistics of wages and hours of labour*, Studies and reports, Series N, No. 2 (Geneva, 1923).

[2] — *International Conference of Labour Statisticians*, Studies and reports, Series N, No. 4 (Geneva, 1924), pp. 30-48.

[3] — International Labour Conference, Twenty-Fourth Session, Geneva, 1938: *Record of proceedings*, pp. 34-35, 292-298 and 646-670.

[4] — *Wages and payroll statistics*, Studies and reports, New series, No. 16 (Geneva, 1949).

[5] — *The Seventh International Conference of Labour Statisticians* (Geneva, 1951), pp. 16-30 and 53-54.

[6] — *Report of the Committee of Experts on Statistics of Hours of Work* (Geneva, 1962; mimeographed).

[7] — *Statistics of hours of work*, Tenth International Conference of Labour Statisticians, Report III (Geneva, 1962; mimeographed).

[8] — *Tenth International Conference of Labour Statisticians 1962* (Geneva; mimeographed), pp. 19-23 and 57-61.

[9] — *Report of the Meeting of Experts on Statistics of Wages and Labour Costs* (Geneva, doc. MELC/D.2/1964; mimeographed).

[10] — *Statistics of labour costs*, Eleventh International Conference of Labour Statisticians, Report II (Geneva, 1966; mimeographed).

[11] — *The Eleventh International Conference of Labour Statisticians 1966* (Geneva; mimeographed), pp. 6-12 and 39-44.

[12] — *Report of the Committee of Experts on Statistics of Wages and Employee Income* (Geneva, doc. WEI/1968/V; mimeographed).

[13] — *Statistics of wages and employee income*, Twelfth International Conference of Labour Statisticians, Report II (Geneva, 1973; mimeographed).

[14] — *The Twelfth International Conference of Labour Statisticians 1973* (Geneva, 1974; mimeographed), pp. 10-14, 18-25 and 35.

Texts

A. Resolution concerning statistics of wages and hours of labour adopted by the First International Conference of Labour Statisticians (October-November 1923)

Detailed statistics of rates of wages, of actual earnings, and of normal and actual hours of labour should be collected and published in each country as frequently as possible, account being taken of the special circumstances and conditions obtaining in each case. With a view to facilitating international comparisons, the responsible authorities in each country should, as far as practicable, observe the following principles:

(1) At regular intervals, and at least once a year, there should be published—

(a) statutory minimum rates;

(b) rates fixed in collective agreements;

(c) rates accepted by organisations of employers and workpeople for typical categories of workers.

(2) In order to provide an indication of the general course of wage movements, information should be published at more frequent intervals as to the nature and amount of any changes resulting from alterations in the statutory minimum rates or arranged between organisations of employers and workpeople. Particulars should be given of changes in the normal hours of labour and of alterations in the level of piece-work rates.

(3) At regular intervals, not less than once a year, average actual earnings and actual hours of labour during a year or a typical period in a year should be given for each of the principal industries, and based on data supplied by representative employers or establishments.

(4) From the data indicated above, index numbers should be computed to show the general course of changes in nominal wage rates and in actual earnings. Index numbers of the purchasing power of the wages should also be calculated by relating changes in actual earnings to changes in the cost of living, the necessary precautions being taken to ensure that the two series of data are comparable.

The nominal wages employed in computing the index numbers should be given in every case.

(5) At less frequent intervals general wage censuses should be taken, information being obtained from the pay sheets of establishments to show rates of wages and the actual earnings in a typical week. The information should be given by industries, districts, occupations and sex, and a distinction should be made between adults and young persons.

Until the principles enunciated above have been applied in the different countries, statistics of wages and hours of labour should at least give—

(a) current rates of wages (hourly or weekly) and normal hours of work of typical categories of time workers; and at regular intervals averages weighted according to the number of workers to whom the data apply both for such categories and for all categories combined;

(b) actual and full-time earnings and hours of labour for typical categories of workers, especially those paid on piece work; such statistics should be available for sample periods, at least once a year;

(c) real wage index numbers based on nominal-wage and cost-of-living index numbers.

In order that the International Labour Office may make tentative comparisons of the level of real wages in the different countries, the competent statistical authorities of each country should furnish the International Labour Office at regular intervals (if possible monthly) with statements in a form to be agreed upon, showing for the capital cities of their respective countries—

(i) the time-rates of wages and normal weekly hours of labour current in a limited number of typical occupations; and

(ii) information as to the prices of a limited number of those items upon which the income of working-class families in most industrially developed countries is largely spent.

B. Conclusions of the First International Conference of Statisticians convened by the Social Science Research Council of the United States of America (Geneva, January 1929)

INDEX NUMBERS OF WAGES

. . . .

There are three obvious and very distinct purposes for which index numbers of wages may be required:

(1) to determine one of the elements for measuring fluctuations in the standard of living;

(2) to calculate the remuneration per hour of work;

(3) to calculate the labour cost per unit of production.

. . . .

In addition to the three main purposes analysed above, there are two others for which index numbers of wages have been employed. There is, first, that of measuring the variations in the total amount of wages as a percentage of the national income and, secondly, that of using them as one of the factors in economic forecasting. The Committee was of opinion that this latter purpose was particularly important and therefore gave it special attention.

. . . .

The committee did not claim to deal with all the important points, but was content to consider for each type of index—

(1) the wages data (rate of wages, average wages or actual earnings) to be taken into account in each case;

(2) the industries or classes of workers to which these data should refer;

(3) the areas from which returns should be collected;

(4) the period during which the data should be gathered;

(5) the method of arriving at the index numbers, that is, the weighting of the various classes or industries, the choice of the basic period, etc.

. . . .

*I. Construction of indices to measure changes in the standard of living
of the working class as a whole*

(1) Choice of type of wage data

If the standard of living is used in its generally accepted sense of material well-being, it is evident that, for the purpose of constructing wage index numbers to measure changes in the standard of living of the working class as a whole, the ideal type of data to be used should be actual annual earnings, or earnings for a shorter period representative of annual earnings.

Experience in certain countries shows that in fact changes in actual earnings may differ from changes in rates of wages and in average wages per hour. But this does not exclude the fact that in other countries changes in rates of wages may be considered as approximately representative of changes in actual earnings in certain industries and under certain conditions.

While recognising that, in normal conditions, the standard of living may be considered proportional to actual earnings, it must be recognised that changes in hours worked and other social conditions equally affect the standard of living and the accuracy of an index number based on actual earnings. In these cases, it would be desirable to take hours of labour into consideration.

(2) Industries and categories of workers to be included

For the construction of such index numbers it would be desirable to consider changes in the wages of the wage-earning class as a whole; but as in practice this would be rarely possible, it is necessary to select certain industries and categories of workers which would be representative of the wage-earning class. In this case it will be necessary to indicate clearly the industries and categories of workers covered by the statistics.

If it is desired to measure the standard of living of the wage-earning class as a whole it is indispensable to include agricultural workers, as well as workers in industry proper. But as in most countries statistics of the cost of living of agricultural workers are not available, it will be necessary, when one wishes to compare index numbers of wages with index numbers of the cost of living, to consider separately the workers in industry proper.

(3) Choice of districts

Where it would not be possible to cover the whole country, districts should be chosen so as to be representative of the whole country. If adequate consideration is not given to this very important point there is the danger that wage index numbers will be compiled which are not representative of the actual situation, either from the point of view of the levels of wages of the wage-earning class or from the point of view of their changes.

(4) Frequency of compilation

From the point of view of the practical use of these statistics, it would appear reasonable that the frequency of compilation should be determined in relation to the stability of economic conditions, compilation being less frequent when these conditions are more stable.

From the point of view of facility in collecting the statistics and for the purpose of ensuring their accuracy, there may be certain reasons, as is shown by the experience of a number of countries, for the compilation of the statistics at frequent intervals, even when economic conditions are stable.

In any case, it is opportune to determine frequency of compilation in relation to the systems of wage payment in use in the different countries, selecting periods for which the wage payments may be considered complete. Generally a period of one month (or four weeks) would appear to be the most suitable and to be satisfactory in relation to other general uses of the wage index numbers. Where the supply of information depends on the good will of the employers, it is necessary to take care that the statistics for successive periods relate to the same establishments. If this condition cannot be realised, it would become necessary to obtain also statistics for the preceding period in order to enable the figures for successive periods to be connected by the chain method.

When a system of payment includes supplementary items of remuneration that cover more than one period of normal payment, it is necessary to allocate such items proportionately among the normal periods that they cover or to average them over the whole period intervening between one such supplementary payment and the next.

(5) Method of compilation

As to the method used in establishing these index numbers, the most precise consists in relating the total actual earnings compiled or calculated for a given period to the corresponding actual earnings for the period taken as base. These averages may be compiled per worker, or better, per member of the family, if it is possible to include the earnings of other members of the family.[1] The last consideration, which may be important in international comparisons, does not, however, have any appreciable effect on time comparisons in a country.

The calculation of a simple or a weighted average index number for the various industries and occupations, the weights remaining constant during the various periods, may lead in certain circumstances to false conclusions, for they do not take into account the movement of workers from one industry to another and from one occupation to another. These movements may in certain cases be of great importance. In consequence it may be necessary to use separate indices for the different industries, and in combining them to revise the weighting as often as possible so as to take account of these changes. For such a series of index numbers the choice of base period does not influence the index number.

. . . .

II. Construction of index numbers of wages for measuring, in each country, the changes in the fluctuation in the standard of living in different industries or occupations

It is of interest for certain purposes to measure fluctuations in the standard of living, not of the workers as a whole, but in different industries or occupations, without taking into account fluctuations in the standard of living of the workers as a whole, which may arise from variations in the numerical importance of different industries or occupations. In this case the same methods are to be recommended as to the choice of wage data, of localities and of periods.

III. Calculation of index numbers of wages as an aid in forecasting economic conditions

(1) Choice of data

In countries which do not possess well organised statistics of unemployment, overtime and short time, or in countries where the wage rates are fixed for a determined

---

[1] These averages will usually be compiled per earner, but when it is possible to obtain the information they may also be compiled per family. In this case the average size of the family should be given, expressed, if possible, in terms of "adult men".

and fairly lengthy period, the statistics of earnings have advantages for following economic fluctuations. In countries for which the statistics of unemployment, etc. are well organised, and where rates of wages can be changed according to economic conditions, it may be useful to consider rates of wages also as an index for economic forecasting, as at the beginning of a crisis these rates may vary according to the orders received by establishments, and consequently may constitute a more sensitive index than that of actual earnings.

(2) Industries and categories of workers

In every country it is necessary to take into consideration the industries and categories of workers whose variations in wage rates or actual earnings are the most sensitive; the work of choosing the industries and categories most appropriate for these studies must be left to the specialists of each country. Certain industries even of less economic importance, like the luxury trades and printing, may give interesting information in this field, whilst industries which receive orders long periods in advance, and may in certain cases be the most important ones from the economic point of view, may be less suitable for forecasting.

In each branch of industry the best organised establishments which can estimate with the greatest certitude the future development of the market should primarily be considered.

(3) Choice of localities

In order to establish economic forecasts it is advisable to take into special consideration certain centres or localities which, either because of the concentration of industry, or because of some special development, or for other reasons, are, as experience has shown, the first to show symptoms of crisis or of economic revival.

(4) Frequency

The interval chosen should be as short as possible.

(5) Method of compilation

It would be advisable, even if it were desired to reduce the various information into one index, to publish separately the information for the various industries, occupations, and localities, so that all necessary information would be available for the interpretation of these indices.

IV. Compilation of index numbers of wages to measure earnings per hour in respect of work of comparable character and efficiency

(1) Choice of data

It may be assumed that the best method theoretically would be to determine separately the average wages per hour of normal work and the average wages per hour of overtime, and then to eliminate the influence of varying amounts of overtime by combining these two averages in a constant ratio.

As in many countries it is not possible in practice to distinguish between normal and overtime earnings, the most practical method is to calculate a single average by dividing the aggregate amount of actual earnings—for normal and overtime work, including special allowances, payments in kind, etc.—by the total number of hours worked. The objection to this method of calculation is that changes in the payment per hour worked may result from a mere change in the proportion of overtime worked to normal hours; this objection being the more important, the more significant the changes in this proportion.

45

(2) Industries and categories of workers

The comparison aimed at is one between certain categories of workers belonging to selected occupations who work with approximately similar equipment and under similar conditions in different countries or in different periods. It must be recognised, however, that the individual workers who perform the same occupations in different countries and in various periods may diverge in varying degrees from the average worker in respect to individual skill and efficiency. This objection will be the more important in practice, the more restricted the number of occupations and the number of workers considered.

Even if the comparisons between different countries may on this account be open to doubt, it may well be that the variations in time shown by these index numbers may be comparable.

(3) Localities

It may be assumed that the localities should be representative of the conditions of the whole country. Consequently it may not be sufficient to limit the statistics to capital or principal cities, because the differences in this respect between these and the rest of the country may be more or less great according to the country or the period considered.

(4) Frequency

If it were possible to determine separately the average wages per normal hour and per hour of overtime, it would be desirable to secure data as frequently as possible. Since in general such data are not available, it will be necessary to take rather long intervals so that the different circumstances influencing the amount of overtime work might arrange themselves out.

(5) Method of calculation

It goes without saying that the different occupations chosen for international comparisons will comprise different numbers of workers in different countries, and that these differences will not be similar in all countries and will even present considerable variations from country to country.

Since the index numbers are to be used to measure the changes in the earnings per hour of work of a given nature and given efficiency, it will be necessary to calculate as many special index numbers as there are from this point of view different categories, and then to compute an average of these index numbers.

It is evident that the index numbers calculated for different categories of workers should be weighted according to the number of workers in each category. A practical difficulty in comparing the index numbers in different countries arises from the fact that the numbers of workers of each category would vary from country to country, and that there is no reason for taking as basis the number of workers in one country rather than that in another country. In order to avoid this difficulty it might be advisable to repeat the calculation as many times as there are countries, using in turn the weight corresponding to the conditions prevailing in each country.

The results of the calculation will show whether the application of the different methods of weighting will produce significant deviations.

V. Compilation of index numbers of wages for the purpose of measuring the labour cost per unit of production

If the unit of production is taken in the sense of a unit of value, the determination of labour cost per unit of production consists in calculating the percentage of the total value of production represented by the aggregate wages paid. It is evident that, even if in some countries and in certain branches of productive activity firms already furnish data of this kind, it is not possible to expect at present an extension of these inquiries over all branches of economic activity and all countries. In this respect the Committee, while hoping that this will be possible in respect to an increasing part of production and increasing number of countries, considers that the collection of data on wages, cost of labour and cost of production should be organised as far as possible so as not to give rise to fears or opposition on the part of the firms concerned. Even if this opposition to supplying such detailed information is sometimes due rather to habits or traditional ideas which are no longer justifiable, it is necessary in any case to take account of them because the sincere collaboration of the heads of firms constitutes an exceedingly useful element in ensuring the accuracy of the data.

. . . .

In compiling these index numbers it is convenient to proceed as follows:

(1) to take as bases the actual earnings—that is to say, the aggregate and not the average earnings;

(2) and (3) if it is not possible to take into account all localities and industries concerned, to choose representative localities and industries;

(4) to obtain records of wages for the same periods as for the censuses or evaluations of production, which can only be effected at rather long intervals;

(5) to adopt for the index numbers of wages the same base as for the index numbers of production, and to follow in respect of weighting the principles specified under I and II, according as it is proposed to make, or not to make, allowance for the effects of differences in the importance of the production of different industries.

VI. Compilation of index numbers of wages for measuring the variations in the proportion of the national income formed by wages

The percentage of the value of production represented by the aggregate wages of labour may have a very different significance according as it applies to primary production (extractive industries, forestry or agriculture) in which the consumption of the products of other industries is of small importance or to manufacturing industries in which an important part of the value of the product is due to raw materials or semi-manufactured products. This inconvenience might be avoided if the total wages are related not to the total value of production but to the value of the net product of industry.

. . . .

As regards the choice of data concerning wages, industries, localities, the frequency of collection, and the methods of calculating the index numbers, the principles indicated under V may in general be applied.

. . . .

C. Conclusions relating to wage index numbers adopted by the Second International Conference of Statisticians convened by the Social Science Research Council of the United States of America (Geneva, May 1930)

1. The construction of index numbers to measure the movement of wages, although designed primarily for use within a country, is of importance also for the international comparison of wages. Any divergence between the movement in two countries is the reflection of a significant change and may be a cause of further change in the economic relations of the two countries. It is important, therefore, that indices of wage movements in different countries should be made available for purposes of

comparison, and the Conference Committee welcomes the initiative of the International Labour Office since the last Conference in publishing together all the available indices of wage movements.

2. The Committee is of opinion that the indices published should take three forms:

(a) It is desirable, whether a single numerical index is compiled or not, that as much as is practicable of the detailed information on which such numerical indices may be based should be published. The problems in the elucidation of which wage statistics are required are so numerous and varied that it is not possible to meet all the needs that may arise. It is, therefore, important that such material as exists should be made available for the use of students, and not merely numerical indices based on this material. Full publication of details is necessary also to prevent misunderstanding and misuse of indices.

(b) A general index, inclusive of as much of the available material for each country as can be obtained regularly, should be constructed, where the material is adequate. The publication of such an index, however, would be dangerous unless accompanied by an indication of the movement of wages in the chief component industrial groups. Such more detailed indices should, where possible, give separately the movement of wages of skilled or unskilled and male and female workers.

(c) A special index should be constructed for each country embodying the movement of wages in certain selected industries for the special purpose of international comparison. This index might be modelled on the index set forth in the American report [1], combining the indices for general manufacturing, railways, building and coal mining. Representative rates for these groups can probably be found among the wage statistics of most countries; but whatever combination is included, it should be restricted to industries in which wages are determined by purely industrial conditions, industries in which wages are influenced by political considerations being excluded.

3. The Committee would call attention to certain desiderata in the presentation of statistics. Where possible actual figures of wage rates or of averages of wage rates should be given, as well as the index or indices of change in wage rates, since it is possible for actual wage rates to remain unchanged, while the index number in which they are combined changes on account of some alteration in the proportion of different classes of workers, or the rise to importance of some hitherto unimportant industry.

Tables should be accompanied by notes warning the reader of the limits within which and purposes for which the figures may be used. References to the official publications of the different countries from which the figures are taken or the indices compiled should always be given.

The Committee wishes to stress the recommendation of the 1929 Conference that statistics of both rates of wages and earnings should be compiled. Pending collection of such comprehensive statistics they recommend that rates and earnings should be given wherever they are available; that it should be made clear whether the figure given represents wages or earnings where only one is available; and that where rates only are embodied in the index the relation between earnings and rates, in the years for which figures of earnings are available, should be given. They suggest also that it may be advisable to omit from any index based exclusively upon rates occupations in which it is known that the divergence between earnings and rates is considerable.

Where possible the data on wages should be compiled and published monthly, as is already done in certain countries. This is necessary to make possible the study of seasonal fluctuations.

---

[1] Report submitted to the Conference.

Both hourly and weekly rates and earnings should be given when possible.

In any industry or occupation in which a large proportion of women is employed it is desirable that a separate index number of women's wages should be compiled. Where only a small proportion of women are employed this would be impracticable; but in this case it should be stated whether the women's rates are included or excluded from the index for the industry or occupation which is given. Statistical authorities should print full and repeated explanations of the principles on which, and the methods by which, any indices which they publish are constructed.

D. Convention (No. 63) concerning statistics of wages and hours of work in the principal mining and manufacturing industries, including building and construction, and in agriculture, adopted by the International Labour Conference at its 24th Session (1938)

The General Conference of the International Labour Organisation,

. . . .

Having determined that, although it is desirable that all Members of the Organisation should compile statistics of average earnings and of hours actually worked which comply with the requirements of Part II of this Convention, it is nevertheless expedient that the Convention should be open to ratification by Members which are not in a position to comply with the requirements of that Part,

Adopts, this twentieth day of June of the year one thousand nine hundred and thirty-eight, the following Convention, which may be cited as the Convention concerning Statistics of Wages and Hours of Work, 1938:

PART I. GENERAL PROVISIONS

Article 1

Each Member of the International Labour Organisation which ratifies this Convention undertakes that

(a) it will compile as required by this Convention statistics relating to wages and hours of work;

(b) it will publish the data compiled in pursuance of this Convention as promptly as possible and will endeavour to publish data collected at quarterly or more frequent intervals during the succeeding quarter and to publish data collected at intervals of six or twelve months during the succeeding six or twelve months respectively; and

(c) it will communicate the data compiled in pursuance of this Convention to the International Labour Office at the earliest possible date.

Article 2

1. Any Member which ratifies this Convention may, by a declaration appended to its ratification, exclude from its acceptance of the Convention:

(a) any one of Parts II, III, or IV; or

(b) Parts II and IV; or

(c) Parts III and IV.

2. Any Member which has made such a declaration may at any time cancel that declaration by a subsequent declaration.

3. Every Member for which a declaration made under paragraph 1 of this Article is in force shall indicate each year in its annual report upon the application of this Convention the extent to which any progress has been made with a view to the application of the Part or Parts of the Convention excluded from its acceptance.

Article 3

Nothing in this Convention imposes any obligation to publish or to reveal particulars which would result in the disclosure of information relating to any individual undertaking or establishment.

Article 4

1. Each Member which ratifies this Convention undertakes that its competent statistical authority shall, unless it has already obtained the information in some other way, make inquiries relating either to all, or to a representative part, of the wage earners concerned, in order to obtain the information required for the purpose of the statistics which it has undertaken to compile in accordance with this Convention.

2. Nothing in this Convention shall be interpreted as requiring any Member to compile statistics in cases in which, after inquiries made in the manner required by paragraph 1 of this Article, it is found impracticable to obtain the necessary information without the exercise of compulsory powers.

PART II. STATISTICS OF AVERAGE EARNINGS AND OF HOURS ACTUALLY WORKED IN MINING AND MANUFACTURING INDUSTRIES

Article 5

1. Statistics of average earnings and of hours actually worked shall be compiled for wage earners employed in each of the principal mining and manufacturing industries, including building and construction.

2. The statistics of average earnings and of hours actually worked shall be compiled on the basis of data relating either to all establishments and wage earners or to a representative sample of establishments and wage earners.

3. The statistics of average earnings and of hours actually worked shall—

(a) give separate figures for each of the principal industries; and

(b) indicate briefly the scope of the industries or branches of industry for which figures are given.

Article 6

The statistics of average earnings shall include—

(a) all cash payments and bonuses received from the employer by the persons employed;

(b) contributions such as social insurance contributions payable by the employed persons and deducted by the employer; and

(c) taxes payable by the employed persons to a public authority and deducted by the employer.

Article 7

In the case of countries and industries in which allowances in kind, for example in the form of free or cheap housing, food or fuel, form a substantial part of the total remuneration of the wage earners employed, the statistics of average earnings shall be supplemented by particulars of such allowances, together with estimates, so far as practicable, of their money value.

Article 8

The statistics of average earnings shall be supplemented, so far as practicable, by indications as to the average amount of any family allowances per person employed in the period to which the statistics relate.

Article 9

1. The statistics of average earnings shall relate to average earnings per hour, day, week or other customary period.

2. Where the statistics of average earnings relate to average earnings per day, week or other customary period, the statistics of actual hours shall relate to the same period.

Article 10

1. The statistics of average earnings and of hours actually worked, referred to in Article 9, shall be compiled once every year and where possible at shorter intervals.

2. Once every three years and where possible at shorter intervals the statistics of average earnings and, so far as practicable, the statistics of hours actually worked shall be supplemented by separate figures for each sex and for adults and juveniles; provided that it shall not be necessary to compile these separate figures in the case of industries in which all but an insignificant number of the wage earners belong to the same sex or age group, or to compile the separate figures of hours actually worked for males and females, or for adults and juveniles, in the case of industries in which the normal hours of work do not vary by sex or age.

Article 11

Where the statistics of average earnings and of hours actually worked relate not to the whole country but to certain districts, towns or industrial centres, these districts, towns or centres shall, so far as practicable, be indicated.

Article 12

1. Index numbers showing the general movement of earnings per hour and where possible per day, week or other customary period shall be compiled at as frequent and as regular intervals as possible on the basis of the statistics compiled in pursuance of this Part of this Convention.

2. In compiling such index numbers due account shall be taken, inter alia, of the relative importance of the different industries.

3. In publishing such index numbers indications shall be given as to the methods employed in their construction.

PART III. STATISTICS OF TIME RATES OF WAGES AND OF NORMAL HOURS OF WORK IN MINING AND MANUFACTURING INDUSTRIES

Article 13

Statistics of time rates of wages and of normal hours of work of wage earners shall be compiled for a representative selection of the principal mining and manufacturing industries, including building and construction.

Article 14

1. The statistics of time rates of wages and of normal hours of work shall show the rates and hours—

(a) fixed by or in pursuance of laws or regulations, collective agreements or arbitral awards;

(b) ascertained from organisations of employers and workers, from joint bodies, or from other appropriate sources of information, in cases where rates and hours are not fixed by or in pursuance of laws or regulations, collective agreements or arbitral awards.

2. The statistics of time rates of wages and of normal hours of work shall indicate the nature and source of the information from which they have been compiled and whether it relates to rates or hours fixed by or in pursuance of laws or regulations, collective agreements or arbitral awards, or to rates or hours fixed by arrangements between employers and wage earners individually.

3. When rates of wages are described as minimum (other than statutory minimum) rates, standard rates, typical rates, or prevailing rates, or by similar terms, the terms used shall be explained.

4. "Normal hours of work", where not fixed by or in pursuance of laws or regulations, collective agreements or arbitral awards, shall be taken as meaning the number of hours, per day, week or other period, in excess of which any time worked is remunerated at overtime rates or forms an exception to the rules or custom of the establishment relating to the classes of wage earners concerned.

Article 15

1. The statistics of time rates of wages and of normal hours of work shall give—

(a) at intervals of not more than three years, separate figures for the principal occupations in a wide and representative selection of the different industries; and

(b) at least once a year, and if possible at shorter intervals, separate figures for the main occupations in the most important of these industries.

2. The data relating to time rates of wages and of normal hours of work shall be presented, so far as practicable, on the basis of the same occupational classification.

3. Where the sources of information from which the statistics are compiled do not indicate the separate occupations to which the rates or hours apply, but fix varying rates of wages or hours of work for other categories of workers (such as skilled workers, semi-skilled workers and unskilled workers) or fix normal hours of work by classes of undertakings or branches of undertakings, the separate figures shall be given according to these distinctions.

4. Where the categories of workers for which figures are given are not separate occupations, the scope of each category shall, in so far as the necessary particulars are given in the sources of information from which the statistics are compiled, be indicated.

Article 16

Where the statistics of time rates do not give the rates per hour but give rates per day, week, or other customary period—

(a) the statistics of normal hours of work shall relate to the same period; and

(b) the Member shall communicate to the International Labour Office any information appropriate for the purpose of calculating the rates per hour.

Article 17

Where the sources of information from which the statistics are compiled give separate particulars classified by sex and age, the statistics of time rates of wages and of normal hours of work shall give separate figures for each sex and for adults and juveniles.

Article 18

Where the statistics of time rates of wages and of normal hours of work relate not to the whole country but to certain districts, towns or industrial centres, these districts, towns or centres shall, so far as practicable, be indicated.

Article 19

Where the sources of information from which the statistics of time rates and of normal hours of work are compiled contain such particulars, the statistics shall at intervals not exceeding three years indicate—

(a) the scale of any payment for holidays;

(b) the scale of any family allowances;

(c) the rates or percentage additions to normal rates paid for overtime; and

(d) the amount of overtime permitted.

Article 20

In the case of countries and industries in which allowances in kind, for example in the form of free and cheap housing, food or fuel, form a substantial part of the total remuneration of the wage earners employed, the statistics of time rates of wages shall be supplemented by particulars of such allowances, together with estimates, so far as practicable, of their money value.

Article 21

1. Annual index numbers showing the general movement of rates of wages per hour or per week shall be compiled on the basis of the statistics compiled in pursuance of this Part of this Convention, supplemented, where necessary, by any other relevant information which may be available (for example, particulars as to changes in piece-work rates of wages).

2. Where only an index number of rates of wages per hour or only an index number of rates of wages per week is compiled, there shall be compiled an index number of changes in normal hours of work constructed on the same basis.

3. In compiling such index numbers due account shall be taken, inter alia, of the relative importance of the different industries.

4. In publishing such index numbers indications shall be given as to the methods employed in their construction.

PART IV. STATISTICS OF WAGES AND HOURS OF WORK IN AGRICULTURE

Article 22

1. Statistics of wages shall be compiled in respect of wage earners engaged in agriculture.

2. The statistics of wages in agriculture shall—

(a) be compiled at intervals not exceeding two years;

(b) give separate figures for each of the principal districts; and

(c) indicate the nature of the allowances in kind (including housing), if any, by which money wages are supplemented, and, if possible, an estimate of the money value of such allowances.

3. The statistics of wages in agriculture shall be supplemented by indications as to—

(a) the categories of agricultural wage earners to which the statistics relate;

(b) the nature and source of the information from which they have been compiled;

(c) the methods employed in their compilation; and

(d) so far as practicable, the normal hours of work of the wage earners concerned.

PART V. MISCELLANEOUS PROVISIONS

Article 23

1. Any Member the territory of which includes large areas in respect of which, by reason of the difficulty of creating the neccessary administrative organisation and the sparseness of the population or the stage of economic development of the area, it is impracticable to compile statistics complying with the requirements of this Convention may exclude such areas from the application of this Convention in whole or in part.

2. Each Member shall indicate in its first annual report upon the application of this Convention submitted under Article 22 of the Constitution of the International Labour Organisation any areas in respect of which it proposes to have recourse to the provisions of this Article and no Member shall, after the date of its first annual report, have recourse to the provisions of this Article except in respect of areas so indicated.

3. Each Member having recourse to the provisions of the present Article shall indicate in subsequent annual reports any areas in respect of which it renounces the right to have recourse to the provisions of this Article.

Article 24

1. The Governing Body of the International Labour Office may, after taking such technical advice as it may deem appropriate, communicate to the Members of the Organisation proposals for improving and amplifying the statistics compiled in pursuance of this Convention or for promoting their comparability.

2. Each Member ratifying this Convention undertakes that it will—

(a) submit for the consideration of its competent statistical authority any such proposals communicated to it by the Governing Body;

(b) indicate in its annual report upon the application of the Convention the extent to which it has given effect to such proposals.

PART VI. FINAL PROVISIONS

. . . .

E. Resolution on the Convention (No. 63) concerning statistics of wages and hours of work, 1938, adopted by the Seventh International Conference of Labour Statisticians (September-October 1949)

The Seventh International Conference of Labour Statisticians,

. . . .

Adopts, this seventh day of October 1949, the following resolution:

1. The Conference strongly urges the various countries which have not yet ratified Convention No. 63 to proceed to do so as rapidly as possible.

2. The Conference requests the Governing Body of the International Labour Office to communicate to the Members of the Organisation the proposed Recommendation of the Fifth International Conference of Labour Statisticians containing proposals for the amplification and improvement of the statistics compiled in pursuance of the Convention, together with the following additional proposals:

(a)   (i) for the purpose of statistics of wages and hours of work in different industries, the data to be published should, so far as possible, be on the basis of the United Nations International Standard Industrial Classification of All Economic Activities;

    (ii) statistics should be given for each of the main divisions of that classification;

    (iii) when the classification used is not that of the United Nations, breakdowns by industries should be published in such a way as to enable a reassembling of the data on the basis of that classification;

(b) in presenting statistics of earnings and of hours of work, countries should define the meaning of the term "wage earner" and "salaried employee" and indicate, more particularly, whether working foremen and persons holding positions of management are covered; wherever possible, separate information should be provided for the two latter categories;

(c) countries should, furthermore, specify whether earnings as published include any of the payments shown below; wherever possible, separate information should be published on each one of these payments:

    (i) payments to workers on holiday, on vacation, on sick leave, on strike, and to workers performing their military service:

    (ii) supplements for overtime;

    (iii) bonuses paid regularly;

(d) in accordance with Articles 7 and 8 of the Convention, family allowances and the value of payments in kind, where they exist, should be shown separately;

(e) wherever possible, in complement to the main series, average earnings weighted on a fixed basis, e.g. by using pre-war employment figures, should be computed;

(f) where possible, schedules used for industrial censuses, censuses of distribution, etc. and information derived from the administration of social insurance schemes should be utilised to provide statistics of earnings; in the case of social insurance schemes special inquiries may be necessary to cover the earnings of persons not included in such schemes or to cover that portion of earnings which is above the upper wage limits, where such exist.

ANNEX: PROPOSED RECOMMENDATION SUGGESTED TO THE INTERNATIONAL LABOUR CONFERENCE BY THE FIFTH INTERNATIONAL CONFERENCE OF LABOUR STATISTICIANS (Geneva, October 1937)

Whereas the Convention on statistics of wages and hours of work is necessarily limited in scope to statistics which are sufficiently developed to permit of a substantial number of Members entering into definite obligations in respect thereof; and

Whereas it is of special importance that every effort should be made further to improve statistics of wages and hours of work;

The Conference, with a view to completing the provisions of the statistics of wages and hours Convention, recommends that each Member should give effect to the following provisions:

1. (1) Statistics of time rates of wages and of normal hours of work and/or statistics of average earnings and of hours actually worked should be compiled in

respect of wage earners engaged in transport, commercial or trading establishments, and administrative services.

(2) Statistics of salaries and hours should be compiled for salaried employees, excluding persons holding positions of management.

(3) These statistics should be compiled as far as possible at the intervals specified in the statistics of wages and hours Convention in respect of statistics relating to persons to whom that Convention applies.

2. (1) At least every ten years, statistics of average earnings and of hours actually worked should be compiled for each of the principal occupations in each industry.

(2) These statistics—

(a) should show the number of workpeople grouped according to the amount of their earnings; and

(b) should be given by sex and by age groups.

3. (1) Statistics showing the aggregate amount of wages and salaries paid per annum in each of the principal industries in mining and manufacture, including building and construction, and as far as possible, for other branches of economic activity, should be compiled regularly and where possible at annual intervals, and distinguishing as far as possible between wages paid to wage earners and salaries paid to salaried employees.

(2) An approximate indication should be given of the extent to which the returns are representative of all employed persons.

4. Statistics showing average annual earnings of workers in each of the principal industries in mining and manufacture, including building and construction, and as far as possible for other branches of economic activity, should be compiled at intervals of three years, distinguishing as far as possible between wages paid to wage earners and salaries paid to salaried employees.

5. The statistics of time rates of wages should, so far as possible, be accompanied by indications as to the number of workers covered, as well as by any information which may be available as to the relation between the time rates of wages and actual earnings.

6. The statistics compiled in pursuance of this Recommendation should be published and communicated to the International Labour Office as prescribed by the statistics of wages and hours Convention for the statistics compiled in pursuance thereof.

F. Resolution concerning the methods of obtaining statistics of earnings from payrolls adopted by the Seventh International Conference of Labour Statisticians (September-October 1949)

The Seventh International Conference of Labour Statisticians,

. . . .

Being strongly of the opinion that adequate statistics of earnings are essential for the correct appraisal of the economic position of countries and of various social categories within countries,

Being also of the opinion that payroll data provide a suitable basis for the calculation of earnings,

Being further of the opinion that the value of statistics compiled on this basis and their international comparability will be enhanced by the adoption of well defined and uniform methods in the use of payrolls,

Adopts, this seventh day of October 1949, the following resolution:

1. The methods and procedure described in subsequent paragraphs should be adopted in utilising payrolls as a basis for statistics of earnings specified in Convention No. 63 and, where possible, for any other statistics of earnings, including those compiled in accordance with the proposed recommendations of the Fifth International Conference of Labour Statisticians concerning supplementary statistics of wages and hours of work.[1]

2. The methods of obtaining statistics of earnings from payrolls, described below, should also be used, when appropriate, for statistics of earnings which may be derived from other sources, such as censuses of production and distribution, social insurance statistics, etc.

3. Inquiries which are carried out at frequent intervals may be based on returns showing earnings, man-days, man-hours, etc. for broad categories of workers and need not show information for each individual worker.

4. With a view to obtaining accurate information at frequent intervals at minimum cost, consideration should be given to the application of adequate sampling techniques in utilising payrolls for this purpose.

5. (1) In determining a sample of establishments whose payrolls are to be used for the purpose of statistics of earnings, particular attention should be given to securing proper representation of various branches of economic activity, of regions and of establishments of various sizes.

(2) Special efforts should be made to allow for the failure of establishments to make returns.

(3) Studies should be undertaken to determine the best methods for setting up and revising from time to time the list of establishments from which a representative sample is drawn.

(4) Changes in average and total earnings derived from returns from a sample of establishments should, where possible, be applied to benchmark data (taxation returns, industrial censuses, social insurance statistics, etc., these data having been adjusted for this purpose when necessary).

(5) To the extent to which estimates of the total wages and salaries bill are based on average earnings multiplied by employment figures of various groups, such estimates should be adjusted to benchmark data based on more comprehensive returns.

(6) Surveys should be made of the extent to which returns received are in conformity with definitions and instructions contained in the questionnaires.

6. (1) The minimum number of employees for inclusion of an establishment in the sample may vary from industry to industry, but it should be such as to ensure adequacy of representation of each industrial branch covered.

(2) As resources and facilities permit, studies should be undertaken, if necessary, to discover the relationship between trends in earnings in the various size of establishment groups within an industry; if the trends are uneven special care should be taken to ensure that each group is correctly weighted in calculating average earnings for the industry as a whole.

7. In order to comply with the principles of the United Nations International Standard Industrial Classification of All Economic Activities, the basic recording

---

[1] See above, item E.

unit should be the establishment in preference to the undertaking, firm or company; when a single establishment comprises several units engaged in distinct activities, separate returns for each unit should be secured wherever possible.

8. Information should always be made available concerning the criteria used for inclusion of establishments in the sample.

9. Details as to the degree of representativeness of the sample of establishments should be published periodically so as to make possible a fair appraisal of the series.

G. Resolution concerning statistics of hours of work adopted by the Tenth International Conference of Labour Statisticians (October 1962)

The Tenth International Conference of Labour Statisticians,

. . . .

Considering that, in order to improve the statistical methods of each country as well as to permit international comparisons, standard definitions to be used in statistics of hours of work should be set up and existing international recommendations on the methods of collection of data on hours of work should be co-ordinated and developed; Adopt this eleventh day of October 1962 the following resolution:

GENERAL OBJECTIVES

1. This resolution applies to wage earners and salaried employees.

2. Each country should aim to develop a comprehensive system of statistics of hours of work in order to provide an adequate statistical basis for the analysis of conditions of work, the study of trends of economic activity, the analysis of partial employment and of underemployment, the study of productivity, the computation of industrial accident rates and the computation of average hourly earnings.

3. These statistics should be developed in accordance with the specific needs of each country in the light of its social and economic structure and in accordance with international standards, in order to promote comparability among countries. Some countries will encounter difficulties in implementing this resolution at the present stage. These countries should envisage the resolution as a first attempt towards the improvement of international comparability in the field of statistics of hours of work. It is expected that at a later stage the resolution will be revised taking into account the experience gained in its implementation.

DEFINITIONS

4. (1) Normal hours of work are the hours of work fixed by or in pursuance of laws or regulations, collective agreements or arbitral awards.

(2) Where not fixed by or in pursuance of laws or regulations, collective agreements or arbitral awards, normal hours of work should be taken as meaning the number of hours per day or week in excess of which any time worked is remunerated at overtime rates or forms an exception to the rules or custom of the establishment relating to the classes of workers concerned.

5. (1) Statistics of hours actually worked should include—

(a) hours actually worked during normal periods of work;

(b) time worked in addition to hours worked during normal periods of work, and generally paid at higher rates than normal rates (overtime);

(c) time spent at the place of work on work such as the preparation of the workplace, repairs and maintenance, preparation and cleaning of tools, and the preparation of receipts, time sheets and reports;

(d) time spent at the place of work waiting or standing-by for such reasons as lack of supply of work, breakdown of machinery, or accidents, or time spent at the place of work during which no work is done but for which payment is made under a guaranteed employment contract;

(e) time corresponding to short rest periods at the workplace, including tea and coffee breaks.

(2) Statistics of hours actually worked should exclude—

(a) hours paid for but not worked, such as paid annual leave, paid public holidays, paid sick leave;

(b) meal breaks;

(c) time spent on travel from home to work and vice versa.

6. Because of the wide differences among countries with respect to wage payments for holidays and other periods when no work is performed, it does not seem feasible at this time to adopt international definitions of hours paid for. Many countries will find, however, that statistics of hours paid for, while not suitable as a substitute for hours actually worked, can be useful for internal purposes and that they will commonly be readily available from payrolls and other records.

METHODS OF COLLECTION

7. Normal hours of work, where not fixed by or in pursuance of laws or regulations, collective agreements or arbitral awards, should be ascertained from organisations of employers and workers, from joint bodies, or from other appropriate sources of information such as special establishment surveys.

8. In order to allow for international comparisons of normal hours of work between countries where normal hours are fixed by the week and those where they are fixed by the day, countries in which hours of work are fixed by the day should indicate the number of days and half-days usually worked per week in each industry or branch of economic activity.

9. (1) Statistics of hours of work may be collected by establishment surveys or by household sample surveys.

(2) Establishment surveys have the advantage of yielding more accurate results; household sample surveys permit the coverage of a wider section of the working population and also make it possible to obtain indications on total hours worked by each person surveyed, particularly when they have several jobs.

(3) In countries where the majority of establishments are not in a position to supply data on aggregate man-hours worked, data should be collected from each establishment included in the survey on the average number of hours of work per week per worker actually applying to the employees of the establishment; such information may be combined into weighted averages per industry and supply a good substitute for average hours of work obtained by dividing aggregate man-hours by the number of workers.

10. In order to collect accurate data, the forms utilised to collect statistics on hours actually worked should contain detailed instructions as to the categories of hours which should be included or excluded from the data reported.

11. (1) Where the national definition of hours of work differs from the international definition of hours actually worked given in paragraph 5, inquiries should be undertaken from time to time in order to determine the difference between the data collected on the basis of the national definition and those which would have been obtained by using the international definition.

(2) In particular, where the data collected correspond to hours paid for, inquiries should be undertaken from time to time to determine for each industry the ratio between the number of hours actually worked as defined in paragraph 5 and the number of hours paid for.

TABULATION OF DATA

12. (1) Information on normal hours of work should be compiled once a year for each major division of economic activity and, within each division, for each important subdivision.

(2) Statistics of hours actually worked should be compiled at least quarterly for each major division of economic activity (except for agriculture, where the collection of such information frequently involves unusual difficulties) and, within each division, for each important subdivision.

(3) The classification of economic activities used in the compilation of statistics of hours of work should adhere to, or be convertible into, the International Standard Industrial Classification of All Economic Activities.

13. Statistics of hours of work should always cover wage earners; at least once a year, similar data should be obtained for salaried employees, through estimates if necessary.

14. (1) For international comparisons, averages of hours actually worked per worker should preferably refer to a week, taking into account groups laid down in paragraph 15 below; international comparisons on the basis of other reference periods may, however, also prove useful.

(2) Data on hours actually worked originally obtained for periods other than a week should be converted to data referring to a week on the basis of the ratio between the number of working days in the period covered and in a normal week.

(3) Averages of hours actually worked per worker should be obtained by dividing aggregate man-hours by the total number of persons of whom the hours of work have been counted.

15. Where differences in the average number of hours actually worked between important categories of workers are large, separate data on the average number of hours actually worked per worker should be presented for each such category; for instance, for persons working part time, for full-time workers, for those full-time workers who were not absent during the period covered by the statistics, for casual and temporary workers, and males, females and young persons.

16. Data on employment should be collected at least once a year if possible, through establishment surveys or household sample surveys, showing in detail the distribution of persons in employment according to the number of hours they worked during the reference period; for instance, for a reference period of a week, the statistics could show the number of persons who worked 15 hours or less, more than 15 but less than 32 hours, 32 hours, more than 32 but less than 35 hours, 35 hours, more than 35 but less than 40 hours, 40 hours, more than 40 but less than 45 hours, 45 hours, more than 45 but less than 48 hours, 48 hours, more than 48 hours.

17. Data on the number of hours of overtime worked in mining and in each major manufacturing industry should be compiled at least quarterly.

H. Resolution concerning statistics of labour cost adopted by the Eleventh International Conference of Labour Statisticians (October 1966)

The Eleventh International Conference of Labour Statisticians,

. . . .

Considering that international standards for labour cost statistics, particularly as regards definitions, methods of compilation and classification, will promote the development of these statistics along sound lines and contribute to improvement of their international comparability;

Adopt this twenty-seventh day of October 1966 the following resolution:

GENERAL OBJECTIVES AND SCOPE

1. Programmes for statistics of labour cost should be designed essentially to provide reliable measures on the level, composition and evolution of labour cost to the employer. Information collected in labour cost surveys may also be used to throw light on part of workers' income from employment, for instance, direct wages, supplementary wage elements not covered by regular wage statistics, average annual earnings, etc.

2. Each country should aim to develop statistics of employers' labour cost covering the principal sectors of the economy, especially selected branches of manufacturing, mining, building and construction industries, as well as other economic activities where possible.

DEFINITION OF LABOUR COST

3. For purposes of labour cost statistics, labour cost is the cost incurred by the employer in the employment of labour. The statistical concept of labour cost comprises remuneration for work performed, payments in respect of time paid for but not worked, bonuses and gratuities, the cost of food, drink and other payments in kind, cost of workers' housing borne by employers, employers' social security expenditures, cost to the employer for vocational training, welfare services and miscellaneous items, such as transport of workers, work clothes and recruitment, together with taxes regarded as labour cost. The International Standard Classification of Labour Cost given in the annex to this resolution, shows the components of labour cost in more detail.

4. Taxes which are imposed on employment or on payrolls directly affect the cost to employers of employing labour. These taxes, in those countries where they are considered as labour cost, should be identified separately in order that they may be included or excluded for purposes of international comparisons. These taxes should be included on a net basis, i.e. after deduction of any rebates or allowances made by the State.

COMPARABILITY

5. Some labour cost items, as a whole or in part, for example, social security and vocational training, in certain countries are not chargeable to employers, but represent expenditures by the State for social or other reasons. This must be taken into account in making international comparisons.

CLASSIFICATION

6. (1) Labour cost data should be classified by economic activity and, wherever possible, distinguishing wage earners and salaried employees.

(2) Managerial staff remunerated predominantly by a share of profits should be excluded from labour cost statistics.

(3) In the absence of international standard definitions, wage earners and salaried employees should be distinguished according to the criteria most suitable for statistical operations in the country concerned.

7. The classification by economic activity should be in as much detail as possible and should be made according to the United Nations International Standard Industrial Classification of All Economic Activities, or according to a classification convertible into it.

8. (1) Labour cost data should be classified so as to distinguish, wherever possible, at least the major groups of the annexed International Standard Classification of Labour Cost.

(2) It is desirable to prepare separate data for each minor group for which information can be obtained.

(3) Major groups I to IV correspond closely to earnings as compiled by many countries complying with the provisions of Convention No. 63 and may be called "direct labour cost" as distinct from the remaining items which may be called "indirect labour cost". Particular interest attaches to this subdivision of total labour cost.

9. Where statistics pertaining to labour cost exclude major or minor groups covered by the International Standard Classification, this should be indicated, together with estimates of the magnitude of the costs excluded, so far as possible.

10. In the International Standard Classification of Labour Cost annexed to this resolution, the wages and salaries of all personnel, comprising those engaged in activities such as housing, vocational training, medical care and health services, canteens, etc. are included in major groups I to IV and the cost of social security for this personnel is included in major group VI. Consequently, the costs as shown in the other major groups for these activities do not include the wages and salaries (including social security contributions) for personnel of the establishment running these services since many countries may find considerable difficulty in allocating such payments to the appropriate activities. However, in view of the importance in many countries of vocational training, housing and medical care and health services, countries may wish to compile in addition the total cost of these activities, where necessary by way of an estimate. In making such an estimate of total cost of vocational training, the wages and salaries (including social security contributions) paid to trainees and apprentices in respect of training hours should be included. Total cost of any one of these activities comprises also any other items which the country may regard as cost to the employer. Such items should be specified.

11. Where possible, additional classifications of labour cost would be useful for analytical purposes, in particular, classifications by size-groups of establishments, enterprises or firms and by region.

COLLECTION AND COMPILATION

12. The unit for which data are collected should be the establishment, where possible, rather than the enterprise or firm, so far as the accounting system used enables a multi-establishment enterprise to supply data for each establishment.

13. The observation period in comprehensive labour cost surveys should cover the 12 months of the calendar year, whenever possible, otherwise the usual accounting year, to take account of expenditures which occur only annually or irregularly.

14. For each economic activity covered by the national programme of labour cost surveys, it is desirable that data should be collected at intervals not exceeding five years. Until such time as major changes occur in labour cost components, due to

changes in social legislation or other causes, data for the years intervening between two surveys could be estimated wherever suitable data on earnings and other elements of labour cost are available. Special investigations of limited scope during the interim period may provide a satisfactory basis for estimates of certain components of labour cost.

15. Labour cost statistics should be supplemented by employment data of the same scope, showing the number of each sex employed respectively, for instance, as wage earners, salaried employees and, where appropriate, apprentices.

16. Each country should compile statistics of average labour cost per unit of time (cost of labour input). In particular, data should, wherever possible, be compiled showing average labour cost per hour actually worked.

17. For the computation of average labour cost per hour data on man-hours actually worked should be compiled in accordance with the Resolution concerning Statistics of Hours of Work adopted by the Tenth International Conference of Labour Statisticians, 1962 [1], if necessary, by way of an estimate.

18. Wherever possible, data on man-hours worked should be obtained directly in the labour cost inquiry or from other inquiries with a similar coverage.

19. Employers should be given sufficient advance notice of comprehensive labour cost surveys to become familiar with the problems of the survey and be able to adjust their accounting accordingly.

PUBLICATION

20. (1) A description of the concepts and methods used in any important new national labour cost inquiries should be published by the responsible statistical office.

(2) The description should indicate the difference (if any) between the classification of labour cost by components utilised in the national survey and the International Standard Classification.

(3) The methodological description should:

(a) mention the types of bonuses (if any) which have been regarded as wages and included in the national labour cost data relating respectively to direct wages and salaries and to remuneration for time not worked;

(b) give a description of any profit-sharing bonuses included in the national inquiry;

(c) indicate the nature of taxes included.

(4) To facilitate analysis of the data, especially at the international level, the major report of the results of the national inquiry of the labour cost to the employer should give particulars of the national system of financing statutory social security schemes for workers and, more especially, of the proportion of the cost covered by employers' contributions. Information should also be given on welfare services provided for workers by the State.

21. Countries which have made studies of the structure of wages and salaries and other elements of labour cost should communicate their results to the International Labour Office in order to facilitate international comparisons and interpretations of statistics of labour cost.

---

[1] See above, Text G.

ANNEX: INTERNATIONAL STANDARD CLASSIFICATION OF LABOUR COST

I. Direct wages and salaries:

(1) straight-time pay of time-rated workers [1];

(2) incentive pay of time-rated workers;

(3) earnings of piece workers (excluding overtime premiums) [1];

(4) premium pay for overtime, late shift and holiday work.

II. Remuneration for time not worked:

(1) annual vacation, other paid leave, including long-service leave;

(2) public holidays and other recognised holidays;

(3) other time off granted with pay (e.g. birth or death of family members, marriage of employees, functions of titular office, union activities);

(4) severance and termination pay where not regarded as social security expenditure.[2]

III. Bonuses and gratuities:

(1) year-end and seasonal bonuses;

(2) profit-sharing bonus;

(3) additional payments in respect of vacation, supplementary to normal vacation pay and other bonuses and gratuities.

IV. Food, drink, fuel and other payments in kind.

V. Cost of workers' housing borne by employers:

(1) cost for establishment-owned dwellings [3];

(2) cost for dwellings not establishment-owned (allowances, grants, etc.);

(3) other housing costs.

VI. Employers' social security expenditure:

(1) statutory social security contributions (for schemes covering: old-age, invalidity and survivors; sickness, maternity; employment injury; unemployment; and family allowances);

(2) collectively agreed, contractual and non-obligatory contributions to private social security schemes and insurances (for schemes covering: old age, invalidity and survivors; sickness, maternity; employment injury; unemployment; and family allowances);

(3) *(a)* Direct payments to employees in respect of absence from work due to sickness, maternity or employment injury, to compensate for loss of earnings;

   (b) other direct payments to employees regarded as social security benefits;

(4) cost of medical care and health services [3];

---

[1] Including also responsibility premiums, dirt, danger and discomfort allowances, cash indemnities for meals, sandwiches, etc., payments under guaranteed wage systems, cost of living allowances and other regular allowances which are regarded as direct wages or salaries.

[2] Otherwise these should be classified under VI (5).

[3] Other than wages and salaries for personnel in the provision of the service, e.g. the depreciation on buildings and equipment, interest, repairs and maintenance and other cost, *less* grants-in-aid, tax rebates, etc. received from public authorities and receipts from workers. Capital investment made during the year is to be excluded.

(5) severance and termination pay where regarded as social security expenditure.

VII. Cost of vocational training.[1]

(Including also fees and other payments for services of outside instructors, training institutions, teaching material, reimbursements of school fees to workers, etc.)

VIII. Cost of welfare services :

(1) cost of canteens and other food services [1];

(2) cost of education, cultural, recreational and related facilities and services [1];

(3) grants to credit unions and cost of related services for employees.

IX. Labour cost not elsewhere classified.

(Such as costs of transport of workers to and from work undertaken by employer [1] (including also reimbursement of fares, etc.), cost of work clothes, cost of recruitment and other labour costs.)

X. Taxes regarded as labour cost.

(For instance, taxes on employment or payrolls. Such taxes should be included on a net basis, i.e. after deduction of allowances or rebates made by the State.)

I. Resolution concerning an integrated system of wages statistics adopted by the Twelfth International Conference of Labour Statisticians (October 1973)

The Twelfth International Conference of Labour Statisticians,

. . . .

Recalling the existing international standards of statistics of wages and hours of work contained in the resolutions of the First, Seventh, Tenth and Eleventh International Conferences of Labour Statisticians and in Convention No. 63 concerning statistics of wages and hours of work (1938),

Recognising that the need for reliable information on wages and other forms of employee income has increased in recent years both in developed and in developing countries, particularly for purposes of measuring social and economic progress among the various groups in the population,

Recognising further the need to revise, broaden and integrate the existing standards in order to provide guidelines for the production of comprehensive and mutually consistent statistics of wages (including salaries) and the need to co-ordinate these statistics with other economic and social statistics,

Believing that, while there are differences among the needs of the various countries, international guidelines for an integrated system of wages statistics will promote development of these statistics along sound lines and contribute to improvement of their international comparability,

Adopts this twenty-fifth day of October 1973 the following resolution:

GENERAL OBJECTIVES AND SCOPE

1. Each country should aim to develop its statistical programme in the field of wages, hours of work and related matters to provide information for the various users of the statistics, taking into account particular national needs and circum-

---

[1] Other than wages and salaries for personnel in the provision of the service, e.g. the depreciation on buildings and equipment, interest, repairs and maintenance and other cost. *less* grants-in-aid, tax rebates, etc. received from public authorities and receipts from workers. Capital investment made during the year is to be excluded.

stances. The programme should provide for the needs of users in connection with the measurement of levels of living of employees, wage determination, collective bargaining, social, economic and manpower planning, analysis of economic conditions and market conditions, formulating and implementing wage policies and income policies and studies of income distribution.

2. (i) In order to realise the above objectives, national programmes of wages and related statistics should, in principle, cover all sections of the economy, should be developed within the general framework of an integrated system and should comprise two parts: *(a)* current statistics programme to meet short-term needs and *(b)* non-current statistics programme to provide benchmark data as well as other detailed data to meet long-term and continuing needs.

(ii) In establishing any national programme of wages and related statistics, the collaboration of organisations of employers and workers should be sought.

3. The different items and series of wages and related statistics included in the national programme should be compiled in such a way as to be mutually consistent and to reveal the relationships between them. Consistency with other economic and social statistics should also be ensured to the fullest extent possible.

4. (i) The current statistics programme should cover: *(a)* statistics of average earnings and hours of work (including, if possible, hours actually worked) and *(b)* statistics of time rates of wages and normal hours of work.

(ii) The non-current statistics programme should include: *(a)* statistics of wage structure and distribution and *(b)* statistics of labour cost.

5. Statistics of hours of work relevant to wages statistics should be compiled, so far as possible, in accordance with the comprehensive guidelines given in the Resolution of the Tenth International Conference of Labour Statisticians (1962) concerning statistics of hours of work.[1]

6. Labour cost statistics should be compiled, so far as possible, in accordance with the Resolution of the Eleventh International Conference of Labour Statisticians (1966) concerning statistics of labour cost.[2]

7. In view of the special problems of collection of the data, a separate programme of wages statistics should be drawn up for the agricultural sector, within the scope of the general framework of an integrated system of wages statistics, in accordance with the general recommendations below, so far as they are applicable and, so far as it is practicable to do so, also in accordance with the special recommendations on agricultural wages statistics which follow.

CONCEPTS AND DEFINITIONS

Earnings

8. The concept of earnings, as applied in wages statistics, relates to remuneration in cash and in kind paid to employees, as a rule at regular intervals, for time worked or work done together with remuneration for time not worked, such as for annual vacation, other paid leave or holidays. Earnings exclude employers' contributions in respect of their employees paid to social security and pension schemes and also the benefits received by employees under these schemes. Earnings also exclude severance and termination pay.

9. Statistics of earnings should relate to employees' gross remuneration, i.e. the total before any deductions are made by the employer in respect of taxes, contributions

---

[1] See above, Text G.
[2] See above, Text H.

of employees to social security and pension schemes, life insurance premiums, union dues and other obligations of employees.

10. (i) Earnings should include: direct wages and salaries, remuneration for time not worked (excluding severance and termination pay), bonuses and gratuities and housing and family allowances paid by the employer directly to his employee.

(a) Direct wages and salaries for time worked, or work done, cover: (i) straight time pay of time-rated workers; (ii) incentive pay of time-rated workers; (iii) earnings of piece workers (excluding overtime premiums); (iv) premium pay for overtime, shift, night and holiday work; (v) commissions paid to sales and other personnel. Included are: premiums for seniority and special skills, geographical zone differentials, responsibility premiums, dirt, danger and discomfort allowances, payments under guaranteed wage systems, cost-of-living allowances and other regular allowances.

(b) Remuneration for time not worked comprises direct payments to employees in respect of public holidays, annual vacations and other time off with pay granted by the employer.

(c) Bonuses and gratuities cover seasonal and end-of-year bonuses, additional payments in respect of vacation period (supplementary to normal pay) and profit-sharing bonuses.

(ii) Statistics of earnings should distinguish cash earnings from payments in kind.

Wage rates

11. The data on time rates of wages should relate to an appropriate time period such as the hour, day, week, month or other customary period used for purposes of determining the wage rates concerned.

12. Wage rates should include basic wages, cost-of-living allowances and other guaranteed and regularly paid allowances, but exclude overtime payments, bonuses and gratuities, family allowances and other social security payments made by employers. Ex gratia payments in kind, supplementary to normal wage rates, are also excluded.

13. Statistics of wage rates fixed by or in pursuance of laws or regulations, collective agreements or arbitral awards (which are generally minimum or standard rates) should be clearly distinguished from statistics referring to wage rates actually paid to individual workers. Each of these types of wage rates is useful for particular purposes.

14. Time rates of wages for normal periods of work should be distinguished from special and other rates such as piece rates, overtime rates, premium rates for work on holidays and shift rates.

Wage payments in kind

15. In view of the dual nature of wages as cost to the employer and earnings of the employee, it may be necessary to evaluate wage payments in kind according to both of these concepts.

16. In principle, for earnings statistics, payments in kind should be measured on the basis of the value accrued to the employee, since earnings refer to the remuneration or income of a specified group of employed persons, whereas for statistics of wage rates and labour cost the evaluation should be done on the basis of cost to the employer since these data refer to the cost of units of work time.

17. Evaluation of remuneration received in kind on the basis of retail market prices generally provides a reasonable estimate of the value accrued to the employee. This method is frequently followed when income data, including wages, are collected through household surveys.

18. When earnings data are furnished by the employer, it is generally easier for him to express the money value of any payments in kind which are included as equal to the cost to him of the goods or services concerned but, if the employer is unable to report the actual cost incurred, it is convenient to use producers' selling prices, or wholesale prices. However, to evaluate the levels of earnings of employees, an adjustment should be made for the difference between cost to the employer and retail prices wherever payments in kind are significant.

CURRENT WAGES STATISTICS PROGRAMME

19. The current programme should be designed to provide essential data at frequent intervals in order to measure trends and short-term changes in average earnings, hours of work, time rates of wages and normal hours of work.

20. In determining the scope and content of the current programme, the need for speed in the collection and in the processing of data at reasonable cost should be a major consideration.

21. In determining the scope of particular wages statistics series, the need to permit the computation of a satisfactory index of real wages should be borne in mind. In principle, consumer price data and wages data relating to the same group of the wage-earning population should be obtained for this purpose.

Statistics of average earnings and hours of work

22. The current programme of statistics of average earnings and hours of work should cover all important categories of wage earners and salaried employees in all major economic activities in the country.

23. Statistical inquiries on earnings and hours of work may often be advantageously combined with a current survey of establishments carried out for purposes of employment, using the whole of the sample of establishments or a sub-sample. Some other current surveys may lend themselves to the collection of data on earnings and hours of work.

24. While compilation of statistics of average earnings and hours of work on a monthly basis is desirable, this imposes a heavy burden on establishments and on statistical offices. On the other hand, half-yearly or annual collection of data does not provide adequate indicators of short-term seasonal variations or trends. As a minimum, the current programme should include the compilation of quarterly statistics of average earnings and hours of work.

25. The time reference periods for data and the arrangements for collection of data should reflect the typical conditions of disbursement of earnings by establishments and the usual payroll periods used in the different industries covered by the inquiry.

26. In a quarterly survey, data could be collected for a typical payroll in respect of only one month, or of each month, thus providing in the latter case a monthly series and permitting calculation of quarterly averages.

27. Wherever possible, monthly or quarterly statistics of average earnings should be published excluding irregular or infrequent payments such as year-end, half-yearly and similar bonuses in order that the short-term trend in regular earnings will be reflected.

28. If the national monthly or quarterly statistics of average earnings exclude certain important components, such as the annual or other infrequent payments mentioned above, the current programme of earnings statistics should include the

compilation once a year, wherever possible, of statistics of average earnings including these particular components.

29. For issuing data in national publications, the time unit in which average earnings are expressed, e.g. hour, day, week or month, should depend mainly on how meaningful the figures would be in the country concerned and also on the feasibility of collection of the required data.

30. For purposes of international comparisons, it is desirable to present statistics of average earnings and hours of work on a per week basis. Data on earnings and hours for periods other than a week should be converted to a per week basis by applying the ratio between the number of working days in the period covered and the number in a normal week (including fractions of a day in each case).

31. For certain types of comparisons, statistics of average earnings per hour are preferable since hours of work per day, week or month vary over time and between industries and regions and also from one country to another.

32. In countries which compile statistics of average earnings per hour paid for, information on hours actually worked not being available regularly, additional information should be collected, wherever possible, to determine the ratio between the number of hours actually worked and the number of hours paid for.

33. Wherever the available data permit, the statistics of average earnings and hours of work should be compiled for males and for females, for all employees and for wage earners and salaried employees separately, by industry and by region.

Statistics of time rates of wages and normal hours of work

34. National current statistics programmes should make provision, wherever appropriate, for the compilation of statistics of time rates of wages and normal hours of work covering wage earners in each of the important industries. These statistics may take the form of time rates of wages and "normal" hours of work actually in force in representative establishments or, alternatively, of the rates and normal hours of work fixed by, or in pursuance of, laws or regulations, collective agreements or arbitral awards. The statistics should be compiled in respect of adult males and adult females in important occupations, or groups of closely related occupations, in each of the principal industries. Wherever appropriate, corresponding statistics should be compiled for the principal occupations among salaried employees.

35. For compilation of time rates of wages actually paid by establishments and the corresponding hours of work, sample surveys of establishments normally should be undertaken at yearly intervals in respect of important occupations in the principal industries in the country, wherever the facilities and resources available permit. It is possible to cover the same ground by undertaking an annual cycle of monthly surveys each covering a certain selection of occupational groups. The data thus obtained provide valuable up-to-date information to supplement the results of wage structure and distribution surveys undertaken at longer intervals.

36. Where the statistics of time rates of wages do not give the rates per hour but refer to a day, week or other customary period, the statistics of normal hours of work should relate to an identical period. However, if the data collected refer to days of work, in place of hours, information also should be obtained on the average duration of the working day, for purposes of calculating rates per hour.

STATISTICS OF WAGE STRUCTURE AND DISTRIBUTION

37. Wage structure and distribution surveys, including wage censuses, large-scale ad hoc occupational wage surveys and similar inquiries, provide comprehensive

benchmark data for use in the compilation of current statistics of average earnings, hours of work, time rates of wages and normal hours of work and detailed data permitting the compilation of:

(a) statistics of wage rates, earnings and hours of work of wage earners and salaried employees to indicate wage differentials between branches of industry, geographic regions, occupations, males and females, establishments of different sizes and possibly also age groups, educational levels and types of vocational training or qualifications of employees;

(b) detailed data on the composition and components of earnings and wage rates;

(c) statistics showing the distribution of wage earners and salaried employees according to levels of wage rates, earnings and hours of work respectively, classified by various important characteristics of employees.

38. Sample surveys of establishments generally constitute the most suitable means for collection of data on wage structure and distribution. It is particularly important that the design and size of the sample of establishments be adequate and in particular that all sizes of establishments within the scope of the survey, all industries and regions should be correctly represented.

39. In principle, all categories of wage earners and salaried employees, including full time and part time, permanent and temporary, should be covered in the survey. Information may be obtained in respect of all eligible employees in the selected establishments, or a representative sample of these employees. The information collected concerning each employee should include wage rates, earnings, hours of work, age, sex, occupation and, if possible, education, vocational training or qualifications, period of service and, where desired, other relevant particulars. Managerial staff remunerated predominantly by a share of profits should be excluded.

40. In view of the breadth and complexity of wage structure and distribution surveys, countries which undertake them should normally do so only at three- to five-year intervals.

41. Although a time reference period of one year is ideal for certain data collected in wage structure and distribution surveys, in practice it is usually necessary to select a shorter reference period considered to be sufficiently representative for the purpose of obtaining data on earnings as well as other items.

42. Data on the composition of earnings and wage rates should be consistent with the classification of components of earnings mentioned in paragraph 10. Supplementary information may be collected on the scales for piece rates, overtime rates, premium rates for work on holidays, shift differentials and similar payments.

43. Statistics of wage rates, earnings and hours of work by occupation should be compiled in as much detail as possible.

AGRICULTURAL WAGES STATISTICS

44. The concepts and definitions given above would be generally applicable to the agricultural sector. Such adaptations as may be necessary in particular countries to meet special conditions in agriculture would normally not be of a fundamental character. Although the international definition of labour cost is also applicable to the whole agricultural sector, statistics of labour cost in the traditional sub-sector of agriculture would not be very meaningful since hired labour constitutes only a minor part of total labour input.

45. For purposes of wages statistics, the agricultural sector should comprise major groups 111 (Agricultural and Livestock Production) and 112 (Agricultural Services) of the International Standard Industrial Classification of All Economic

Activities. In certain circumstances, it may be desirable to compile data separately for each of these major groups.

46. As the factors affecting wages, hours of work and other conditions of employment in hunting, trapping and game propagation (major group 113 of the ISIC), forestry and logging (division 12) and fishing (division 13) are generally different from those concerning agriculture, these activities should normally be excluded from the scope of agricultural wages statistics.

47. The definition of "agricultural work" established for the 1970 World Census of Agriculture should be adopted for the purposes of wages statistics, so far as possible. By agricultural work or agricultural activities is meant any farm work or planning necessary to the operation of the holding.

48. Wherever possible, separate data should be compiled for permanent or regular employees and others, such as temporary and casual workers.

49. In developed countries and for the modern agricultural sector in developing countries, statistics of earnings based on payrolls and other records of employers should be collected, using the agricultural holding as the reporting unit. However, agricultural employees, apart from permanent employees, are not necessarily attached to one particular agricultural holding. Notably in developing countries, more especially in the traditional sector of agriculture, prolonged continuous employment with the same employer is relatively rare and, in addition, some workers alternate between working for wages and self-employment, or between agricultural and non-agricultural employment. In such situations, the agricultural holding is not the most suitable reporting unit for collection of certain types of data, especially for comprehensive statistics of average earnings during the year from agricultural employment and for statistics of the corresponding hours worked.

50. Statistics of agricultural wages in the traditional sub-sector may be obtained through household sample surveys. The principal activity criterion should be used for defining agricultural employees. A person would thus be considered to be an agricultural employee if the principal source of the income accrued to him during a specified reference period was agricultural wages.

Programme of agricultural wages statistics

51. National programmes of current and non-current agricultural wages statistics should be developed within the framework of an integrated system covering statistics of earnings, wage rates, hours of work and labour cost, so far as possible. Since the resources required for the production of agricultural wages statistics are substantial, particularly in developing countries, priorities should be carefully determined to ensure smooth and satisfactory progress of the national programme of wages statistics.

52. In the developing countries, in order to take account of the problems specific to them, separate subprogrammes of wages statistics should be developed for traditional and organised agriculture, where different methods and data collection techniques are needed. So far as possible, the data collected in the two sub-sectors should be suitable for combination to produce statistics for the agricultural sector as a whole.

53. Selected statistics should be compiled separately for agricultural employees who are paid wholly in cash, those paid wholly in kind and those paid partly in each medium. In addition, information should be given on the amounts for major components of payments in kind, such as food and housing, which are included in published statistics of average earnings of agricultural employees.

54. Wherever possible, the data should be classified according to occupation and according to broad types of agricultural holdings (dairy, poultry, livestock, field crops, mixed farms, etc.).

Current agricultural wages statistics

55. Since there is seasonal variation in agricultural activity, and since the relative importance of agriculture differs from country to country, the interval for collection of current data on earnings and time worked in agriculture should be determined in the light of the needs of each country. The data should cover all categories of agricultural employees, including those paid wholly in kind. However, those employees whose remuneration is not paid regularly at daily, weekly or monthly intervals (but might consist, for example, of a share of the crop, with or without some cash wages) would have to be excluded from the current statistics of earnings.

56. Where a country has a continuing and frequent household sample survey for obtaining labour force data, additional information might be collected, at a reasonable cost, on earnings of agricultural employees and hours or man-days worked. However, attempts to obtain reliable data from this source, in respect of earnings in agriculture, might encounter sampling and other practical problems.

57. Each country which does not regularly compile current statistics of earnings and hours of man-days worked in agriculture should undertake surveys of time rates of wages actually paid and hours worked in agricultural establishments, preferably at intervals of not more than six months. These surveys should cover the principal occupations in agriculture.

58. Where labour contract rates quoted include both a wage rate and hire charges for the worker's own equipment, implements or working animals, adjustments should be made to exclude the hire charges.

Non-current agricultural wages statistics

59. Statistics of wage structure and distribution and of labour cost should be compiled for the organised sub-sector of agriculture at five-yearly intervals, based on results of surveys of agricultural establishments.

60. Since agricultural holdings commonly employ temporary and casual workers and the total earnings of these persons from agricultural work for the data reference period of a wage structure and distribution survey may not be fully reflected in the payroll records of the establishment, data could be collected from the employees currently working on the holding on any additional earnings they had received in respect of paid work on other agricultural holdings during the reference period.

61. Information on the structure and distribution of earnings and hours of work in the traditional sector of agriculture in developing countries could be obtained through household surveys covering agricultural households, especially large-scale surveys of agricultural labour incomes where data are obtained on earnings throughout the year. It is desirable in large-scale sample surveys of agricultural households to design the sample in such a way as to permit monthly or quarterly estimates to be made of average earnings and hours or man-days worked.

CONSUMER PRICE INDICES

4

The subject of consumer price indices was placed on the agenda of the Second International Conference of Labour Statisticians (1925), for which the ILO had prepared a study on methods [1]. The Conference adopted a resolution focused on the measurement of changes in the cost of living of a given country at different periods and containing some recommendations relating to the scope of the indices, the methods of collection of the data, the weights to be used and the methods of determining these weights (especially on the basis of family living studies) [2].

On the morrow of the Second World War, the subject of cost-of-living statistics was examined by the Sixth International Conference of Labour Statisticians (1947) in the light of methodological advances made during and after the war. The report prepared by the Office dealt with the purposes of cost-of-living indices, the techniques for obtaining and compiling the data and the systems of weighting [3]. The Conference reviewed the subject in full and adopted a resolution covering the various questions studied in the report [4]. This resolution, which superseded the resolution adopted by the Second Conference, refers in particular to the scope and definition of cost-of-living indices and methods of collection of retail prices (see "Texts", item A).

In accordance with the wish expressed by the Ninth International Conference of Labour Statisticians (1957), which, in a resolution that it adopted, called for a study of certain theoretical and practical aspects of the measurement of consumer prices [5], the question of computation of index numbers was submitted again to the Tenth Conference (1962). On the basis of an inquiry carried out among national statistical services, the ILO had prepared a report on concepts and definitions, methodology and national practices; a number of particularly important problems raised by the computation of indices were also studied: quality changes, appearance of new products, sampling accuracy, seasonal influences, etc. [6].

In its resolution (see "Texts", item B), the Conference emphasised that, since consumer price index numbers could not attain their objectives if they did not inspire confidence, the concepts, definitions and methods of measurement on which they were based should be described as fully as possible and that these descriptions should be made available to the public. The resolution lays down international standards relating to the methods to be used in collecting the data on prices and for obtaining suitable weighting factors, while at the same time stressing the need for continuing research on many problems relating both to the concepts serving as a basis for the indices and to the methods of computation [7].

References

[1] ILO: *Methods of compiling cost-of-living index numbers*, Studies and reports, Series N, No. 6 (Geneva, 1925).

[2] — *The Second International Conference of Labour Statisticians*, Studies and reports, Series N, No. 8 (Geneva, 1925), pp. 7-20, 34-37 and 69-70.

[3] — *Cost-of-living statistics*, Studies and reports, New series, No. 7 (Part 2) (Geneva, 1948).

[4] — *The Sixth International Conference of Labour Statisticians*, Studies and reports, New series, No. 7 (Part 4) (Geneva, 1948), pp. 26-34, 42-44 and 60-62.

[5] — *Ninth International Conference of Labour Statisticians 1957* (Geneva; mimeographed), pp. 87-88.

[6] — *Computation of consumer price indices (special problems)*, Tenth International Conference of Labour Statisticians, Report IV (Geneva, 1962; mimeographed). A new edition of this report, which was prepared in 1970 (doc. D.16.1970/X. ICLS/IV/CPI), contains also the conclusions and recommendations of the Tenth Conference.

[7] — *Tenth International Conference of Labour Statisticians 1962* (Geneva; mimeographed), pp. 7-12, 32-36 and 62-63.

Texts

A. Resolution concerning cost-of-living statistics adopted by the Sixth International Conference of Labour Statisticians (August 1947)

The Sixth International Conference of Labour Statisticians,

. . . .

Recognising the importance of an adequate statistical basis for the proper weighting of cost-of-living index numbers, and the need for refining methods and techniques so as to ensure that the indices reflect correctly the movements of actual market prices,

Adopts, this twelfth day of August 1947, the following resolution:

1. (1) The object of cost-of-living index numbers should be to measure the changes over time in retail prices of a given standard of living.

(2) This in practice means that the index should measure the changes in retail prices of a given consumption pattern.

2. (1) The pattern of consumption to which any particular index relates should be clearly defined.

(2) All such index numbers should reflect prices actually charged to consumers.

3. (1) The purposes which may be served by such indices in the post-war period are the measuring of changes over time in retail prices currently charged consumers for—

(a) the pre-war consumption level of a given economic group in specified types of communities;

(b) a post-war consumption level of a given economic group in specified types of communities; or

(c) a consumption level of a given standard taking account of price-induced substitutions and any other substitutions imposed by circumstances, with as close regard to the maintenance of the same standard of adequacy as practicable.

(2) In cases where a post-war consumption level is adopted, the index may—

(a) measure the variations in the cost of maintaining unchanged the pattern of consumption in a specific year or period; or

(b) measure price changes using the current pattern of consumption as a weighting diagram adjusted as necessary to conform to changes in the consumption pattern.

(3) Where a decision is taken to measure the variations in the cost of maintaining unchanged the pattern of consumption in a specific year, the pattern of consumption should be examined, and the weighting diagram adjusted, if necessary, at intervals of not more than ten years to correspond with the changes in the consumption pattern.

4. In countries where it is decided to introduce a new weighting diagram, consideration should be given to splicing the new indices to the old series dating back as far as possible.

5. (1) If possible, separate index numbers should be compiled for different economic and social groups, geographical areas and different family types.

(2) Consideration should be given also to establishing index numbers for economic and social, family and geographical groups other than those covered by the existing indices.

6. (1) In order that the basis of the index may be commonly understood and that there should be general confidence in its accuracy, a statement should be published in respect of any index describing the items included, the weighting system used, the method of calculation and the methods and sources used in the collection of prices, including a brief review of the different types of sources covered, the pricing techniques, the weights assigned to each type, and the sampling methods employed in their selection.

(2) A description should also be given of the group or groups of the population to which the index relates.

7. (1) The effective administration of the price-collecting programme requires the careful selection and training of price collection personnel.

(2) The use of appropriate methods of price verification, such as "check pricing" in which price quotations are verified by means of duplicate prices obtained by different agents or "purchase checking" in which actual purchases of the goods priced are made, is recommended.

8. In a period of price control or rationing, where illegal prices are charged openly to the groups to which the index applies, such prices should be taken into consideration, as well as controlled prices.

9. (1) Prices charged for stale, damaged, shop-soiled or otherwise imperfect goods should be ignored, but otherwise the index should be based on prices actually charged for cash sales.

(2) "Sale" or reduced prices should be taken where they are applied to the bulk of a shop's trade in the specified article and "cut" prices should be taken rather than "list" prices where they are in fact charged.

(3) Discounts should be taken into account if they are automatically given to all customers.

10. (1) Studies of price changes in different geographical units should be made to determine the number and identity of the geographical units required to be covered for a satisfactory average index for a given group.

(2) In particular, it may be possible from such studies to effect economies in the number of returns for a given standard of sampling accuracy.

11. (1) In establishing the weighting diagram for a cost-of-living index for a particular group, individual items priced should be assigned weights corresponding to the consumption expenditures not only on the individual items themselves but also on other articles not priced, in accordance with the principle that the weights for items not priced may be added to the weights for those priced, when the price movements of the latter are representative of the price movements of the former.

(2) In this manner all items purchased by the group covered can be represented in the index, although not all are priced.

12. (1) Every effort should be made to include a suitable representation of fresh, canned, dried and frozen fruits and vegetables in the list of goods priced.

(2) If items cannot be priced in every month of the year, or if price differences between different seasons are substantial, it is not advisable to use uncorrected price figures and/or constant weights all through the year.

(3) Whenever necessary and feasible, account should therefore be taken, in the methods adopted, of the seasonal factors in consumption and prices.

(4) Provision should also be made for taking account of seasonal factors in purchases of clothing, fuel and other items showing seasonal variations.

13. Every effort should be made to include a suitable representation of semi-durable and durable consumer goods in the list of goods priced.

14. The use of small sample studies of consumer purchases in the intervals between the more comprehensive surveys envisaged in paragraph 3 (3) is recommended in order to provide the basis for discovering significant changes in consumption patterns to indicate the need for revisions in the weighting diagrams.

15. In order to promote understanding of the nature and uses of indices of retail prices charged a particular group, the term "cost-of-living index" should be replaced, in appropriate circumstances, by the term "price-of-living index", "cost-of-living price index" or "consumer price index".

B. Resolution concerning special problems in the computation of consumer price index numbers adopted by the Tenth International Conference of Labour Statisticians (October 1962)

The Tenth International Conference of Labour Statisticians,

. . . .

Recalling the resolution adopted by the Sixth International Conference of Labour Statisticians concerning cost-of-living statistics [1] and recognising generally the continu-

---

[1] See above, Text A.

ing validity of the basic principles recommended therein and, in particular, the fact that the consumer price index is designed primarily to measure changes in the level of retail prices paid by consumers,

. . . .

Recognising the need for more accurate measurement of consumer price changes and the advantages attaching to such further standardisation of methods and procedures as it seems possible and desirable to promote at present as well as the importance of research on concepts and methodology;

Adopts this eleventh day of October 1962 the following resolution:

1. Consumer price index numbers cannot attain their objectives if their purposes as measurements of price changes are not understood and if they do not command the confidence of the public. Therefore, the concepts, definitions, and procedures of measurement on which the index numbers are based should be described as fully as possible and such descriptions made available for the information of the public.

2. Revisions of the weighting pattern should be undertaken as often as consumption patterns show significant changes and as frequently as may be needed in view of the importance of the acceptability of the index. In order to ascertain whether a given weighting pattern continues to have current validity, information may be obtained from statistics or estimates of sales at the retail level, national accounts data on personal consumption expenditure and frequent small sample surveys of family expenditures.

3. (1) Family expenditure surveys conducted to provide the weighting factors for consumer price index numbers should be as comprehensive as resources will permit and should take into account differences in family size, income levels, geographical and climatic variations, socio-economic groups and other factors which may have a bearing on expenditure patterns.

(2) The results of the family expenditure surveys should be analysed to show the expenditure patterns for categories of the population with differing characteristics and to assist in revealing those categories for which separate consumer price index numbers may be warranted.

(3) Family expenditure surveys may provide information on types of commodities consumed and sources from which goods and services are obtained, which would be useful in setting up the price collection arrangements.

4. In countries which have comprehensive information concerning private consumption expenditure as a component of national accounts and/or on retail sales, such information can be used to derive a weighting pattern for general consumer price index numbers for the whole population. Since the detail normally available is not sufficient for this purpose, it may be necessary to supplement the information from the national accounts with detailed expenditure data from family expenditure surveys.

5. If continuous sample surveys are being carried out they may be used to establish a frequently (including annually) revised series of weights.

6. It is of advantage in certain cases to base the weights on data relating to more than one year so that the effects of temporary abnormalities on the weighting pattern are reduced.

7. The list of commodities and services for which prices are collected and the list of markets, retail stores, service establishments and other outlets from which prices are obtained should be inclusive enough to provide price index numbers representative of the consumption of each of the population groups (including the total population) for which index numbers are calculated.

8. (1) The accuracy of consumer price index numbers depends to a major extent on the accuracy of the price information collected and may be affected both by sampling error and by response or procedural error. Accuracy also depends on the sample of items included and of the prices collected. Every practicable means should be employed to identify the sources of error and to overcome them.

(2) Efforts should be made to ensure that samples of cities or areas, of dwelling units, of sales outlets, and of items priced are as representative as possible of the universes they represent. Probability sampling, although involving difficult practical problems, will normally enhance the accuracy of the price index and, moreover, will make possible an estimate of the sampling error.

(3) As a means of reducing response or procedural errors, standard methods for collecting and processing price data should be developed. Items to be priced should be identified by adequate specifications. Price data should refer to actual transaction prices as distinguished from asking, advertised or list prices.

(4) The outlet samples should be revised as frequently as necessary to take into account variations in the price level resulting from changes in the structure and methods of distribution.

(5) The list of varieties priced should be revised as frequently as may be required to ensure that these varieties continue to be representative of actual purchases.

9. Consumer price index numbers should rest on comparison of identical or equivalent qualities of commodities priced at different times. In order that this condition may be fulfilled, efforts should be made to reduce as far as possible the effect of appreciable quality changes on price comparisons.

10. Consideration should be given to the introduction of new commodities into the index when such items have attained consumer acceptance. New commodities and services should be introduced into the consumer price index only after they have become a significant continuing element of expenditure.

11. (1) In dealing with the problem of seasonality which involves individual commodities subject to substantial shifts in price and consumption during the year, including the periodic disappearance of commodities at certain times of the year, consideration may be given to the use of seasonally varying weights for individual commodities and/or seasonally adjusted price relatives. However, these procedures are difficult and there is considerable variation in their application.

(2) Attention should be given to the development of seasonal adjustment factors with the objective of analysing and permitting the elimination of seasonal patterns in the price index numbers.

(3) For those commodities the prices of which are subject to violent changes over very short periods, e.g. a week or a month, consideration should also be given to collecting prices on two or more occasions during the pricing period and using the average of these prices in the calculation of the index.

12. Although use or consumption value constitutes a possible approach to the derivation of weights for consumer durable goods (other than owner-occupied housing), the weights of such goods generally correspond either to their full purchase value (net of trade-ins) or to the total outlay (including both cash purchases and instalments paid) by the reporting consumers during the family expenditure survey period.

13. (1) A consumer price index should include a component for shelter.

(2) Where the shelter component of a consumer price index is intended to cover only the rent of rented dwellings, the weight should be the ratio of the reported total tenant shelter expenditure to total consumption expenditure.

(3) Where the rent index is being used to measure the price element of both rented and owner-occupied dwellings, the appropriate weight may be derived from reported tenant shelter expenditure and either an increment of rent expenditure to cover the cost of owner-occupancy or the expenditure on operating costs, such as maintenance, repairs, taxes and water charges and possibly other expenditures associated with home ownership.

(4) In certain cases, particularly when owner-occupancy, besides being important, corresponds to housing of a type which is not comparable to rented dwellings and if prices and operating costs of owner-occupied houses do not move parallel with rents, direct measurement of such housing costs may be desirable.

(5) Rents should be priced through a representative sample of all dwellings rented by the index population. Data from successive samples should be incorporated in the index in such a way as to ensure that comparisons are made between houses of similar size, age, built-in facilities and services, location, etc.

14. The consumer price index may include changes in the cost of insurance coverage on consumers' properties. The weights used for this component should be based on total premium payments for these types of insurance, less claims paid, and the price indicator should be the premium rates for fire, theft and other applicable types of insurance, adjusted for the price changes of the physical properties being insured.

15. Continuing research is needed at the national and international levels on many important and complicated problems, both of concept and methodology, in the calculation of consumer price index numbers, particularly in the case of—

(a) methods for eliminating the effects of quality changes and the introduction of new commodities;

(b) the problems posed by seasonal changes in price and consumption;

(c) the concepts and techniques to be used for both weighting and pricing durable consumer goods, including housing;

(d) the treatment of taxation;

(e) the inclusion or exclusion of interest and of certain types of insurance;

(f) the techniques of linking differently weighted index price series.

The International Labour Office should encourage and facilitate such research and the exchange between countries of research and practical experience in these difficult areas of consumer price index construction.

FAMILY LIVING STUDIES

5

The subject of family living studies, which had been approached indirectly by the Second International Conference of Labour Statisticians (1925) in connection with consumer price indices, was included in the agenda of the Third Conference (1926), for which an ILO study on methods [1] had been prepared. In the resolution that it adopted, the Third Conference made recommendations concerning the periodicity of family living studies, the selection of families, the reference period, the details to be recorded and the presentation of the results [2].

In the course of the years that followed, the ILO carried out a programme of analysis and publication of the results of family living studies. All the material available on the methods used was brought up to date for publication in 1940 of a revised study of the subject [3].

After the Second World War, the subject of family living studies was taken up anew in 1949 by the Seventh International Conference of Labour Statisticians, for which the Office had prepared a report on methods [4]. Taking into account the progress achieved since the Third Conference, the Seventh Conference adopted a resolution defining the objectives of family living studies and setting new international standards as regards the organisation of inquiries and the analysis and presentation of the results. The Conference also entrusted to the ILO certain tasks in the field of family living studies and, in particular, proposed the formation of a group of experts to study the problems of making family living studies in less developed areas [5].

In 1953 the United Nations, acting jointly with the International Labour Organisation and UNESCO and in co-operation with FAO and WHO, convened a Committee of Experts on International Definition and Measurement of Standards and Levels of Living. That Committee emphasised that it was highly desirable to organise family living studies whereby real living conditions could be appraised directly and completely.

Following upon the recommendations of that Committee and of the Seventh International Conference of Labour Statisticians, the ILO convened in 1955 a group of experts on family living studies. The group studied the objectives of the inquiries, more particularly with regard to living conditions, consumption and savings; it submitted recommendations on the composition of samples of households, the organisation of the surveys, the collection of data and the special problems raised by the conduct of inquiries in less developed areas [6].

In view of the increasing importance of the role played by statistics of household income and expenditure in economic and social planning, the ILO convened in 1967 a new meeting of experts to study existing international standards relating to inquiries into family expenditure and to submit if need be proposals for amending or broadening those standards. The meeting submitted a report containing a series of recommendations completing and bringing up to date previous recommendations on the objectives and scope of the inquiries, the concepts and basic definitions, as well as the methods of collecting the data and of classifying and presenting the statistics [7].

In 1973 the Twelfth International Conference of Labour Statisticians considered the whole question anew on the basis of a report drafted by the Office [8, 9]. In the resolution that it adopted (see "Texts", item A), the Conference noted first of all that recommendations relating to household income and expenditure surveys should be consistent, so far as possible, with the standards concerning statistics of households that are applied within the System of National Accounts, the Balance of National Economy and the Complementary System of Distribution of Income, Consumption and Accumulation adopted by the United Nations Statistical Commission. The resolution defines the objectives of the surveys and contains a series of recommendations on their periodicity, scope and organisation: basic concepts and definitions, methodology, classifications, tabulation and presentation of the results.

References

[1] ILO: *Methods of conducting family budget enquiries*, Studies and reports, Series N, No. 9 (Geneva, 1926).

[2] — *The Third International Conference of Labour Statisticians*, Studies and reports, Series N, No. 12 (Geneva, 1926), pp. 12-37, 92-98 and 110-112.

[3] — *Methods of family living studies: Income—Expenditure—Consumption*, Studies and reports, Series N, No. 23 (Geneva, 1940).

[4] — *Methods of family living studies*, Studies and reports, New Series, No. 17 (Geneva, 1949).

[5] — *The Seventh International Conference of Labour Statisticians* (Geneva, 1951), pp. 31-40, 54-60 and 66-68.

[6] — *Report of the Working Group of Experts on Family Living Studies* (Geneva, doc. FL/20, 1955; mimeographed).

[7] — *Report of the Meeting of Experts on the Scope, Methods and Uses of Family Expenditure Surveys* (Geneva, doc. FES/1967/VII; mimeographed).

[8] — *Scope, methods and uses of family expenditure surveys*, The Twelfth International Conference of Labour Statisticians, Report III (Geneva, 1971; mimeographed).

[9] — *Twelfth International Conference of Labour Statisticians 1973* (Geneva, 1974; mimeographed), pp. 14-17 and 26-34.

Text

Resolution concerning household income and expenditure surveys adopted by the Twelfth International Conference of Labour Statisticians (October 1973)

The Twelfth International Conference of Labour Statisticians,

. . . .

Recognising the need to revise and supplement the recommendations contained in the Resolution of the Seventh International Conference of Labour Statisticians concerning Methods of Family Living Studies, with a view to promoting the development and use of these statistics along sound lines and also with a view to promoting improvement in their quality and international comparability,

Recognising also that, in the interests of promoting the co-ordination and integration of international statistical standards, new recommendations concerning surveys which provide household income and expenditure statistics should be consistent, so far as possible, with other standards concerning statistics of households, including those within the System of National Accounts, the Balance of National Economy (MPS) and the Complementary System of Distribution of Income, Consumption and Accumulation,

Adopts this twenty-sixth day of October 1973 the following resolution:

OBJECTIVES, FREQUENCY AND SCOPE

1. Statistics drawn from household income and expenditure surveys usually serve one or more of the following objectives, although the difficulties inherent in collecting data make it unlikely that more than a few of these purposes could be served by a single survey:

(a) to obtain weights and other useful data for planning price collection or the construction or revision of consumer price indices, indices of comparative costliness, etc.;

(b) to supply basic data needed for policy making in connection with social and economic planning, and to facilitate determination of needs or the establishment of targets;

(c) to provide data for assessing the impact on household living conditions of existing or proposed economic or social measures, particularly changes in the structure of household expenditures and in household consumption;

(d) to provide data for estimating the redistributive effects of direct and indirect taxation, and of a wide range of social benefits, on the situations of the various types of family;

(e) to analyse the variations in levels of living over a period of years and the disparities among households in the different socio-economic groups, geographic areas, rural and urban zones, etc.;

(f) to supplement the data available for use in compiling official estimates of household accounts in the systems of national accounts and balances;

(g) to furnish data on the distribution of household income and expenditure;

(h) to provide information on particular aspects of living conditions of the population, such as those relating to food consumption, housing and health.

2. Data derived from household income and expenditure surveys may also be used in connection with the determination of minimum wage levels, assessment of the need for revision of minimum wages and other questions relating to wage determination.

3. As a survey may serve more than one of the purposes listed in paragraph 1, it is desirable to ensure that the survey is designed and executed taking into account also the particular requirements, as regards types of data, of secondary users of the survey results.

4. National programmes may consist of continuing surveys with or without infrequent large-scale surveys. As a minimum, a major sample survey of household income and expenditure, so far as possible representing all private households in the country, should be undertaken in each country at intervals not exceeding ten years. Under conditions such as rapid industrial expansion and migration from rural to urban areas, which bring significant changes in the economy and in real income, the surveys should be taken at intervals much shorter than ten years. In general, the developing countries tend to experience a more acute need for up-to-date data of the type provided by household income and expenditure surveys and an interval of not more than five years between surveys would be more appropriate in such countries.

5. (i) If a continuing survey is undertaken covering the full range of investigation of a major survey, but with a smaller annual sample, the average of the results of several successive years of such a continuing smaller-scale survey may provide a satisfactory substitute for a large-scale survey, in respect of data needed for certain applications.

(ii) Smaller-scale surveys should be undertaken in each country during the interval between two large-scale surveys to provide data for use in estimating changes in important aggregates derived from infrequent large-scale surveys.

6. (i) In principle, data should be obtained from households or from other sources on the components of, as well as on the aggregates of, household income and expenditure and on the composition of the household, including in particular the following:

(a) aggregate household income (before deduction of social insurance contributions and taxes) and such details of income as it may be feasible and practical to collect, including information on income of individual members of the household;

(b) direct taxation, fees and other charges not regarded as consumption expenditure and similar transfer payments;

(c) contributions by households to social security schemes and related premiums for insurance contracts providing benefits such as sickness and maternity benefits; old-age, invalidity and survivors' pensions; loss of employment and employment disability compensation; and assimilated benefits;

(d) details of other household expenditures and consumption;

(e) information on the membership of the household;

(f) employment particulars relating to the head of the household (or the chief income earner, if not the head) and other members of the household.

(ii) The following information should also be collected from households, so far as possible:

(a) particulars of the dwelling inhabited by the household;

(b) inventory of selected household durable goods and other property;

(c) outlays for investments, net changes over the reference period in savings and in household or personal liabilities;

(d) other data relating to aspects of the situation of the family and its mode of living of particular interest for analyses of data obtained in surveys of household income and expenditure.

7. Household expenditure data provide valuable information for analysis of the food consumption and the dietary and nutrition situation of households but, in order to throw more light on these matters, a special diet and nutrition inquiry may be carried out concurrently with the household expenditure survey, perhaps using a sub-sample of the survey sample or an independent but closely correlated sample.

ORGANISATION OF SURVEYS

8. To carry out household income and expenditure surveys and various other sample surveys, it is desirable that each country establish a sample survey unit. Such a unit would make provision for expert services in designing and selecting samples, training of interviewers, organisation of survey field work, editing and processing of data. Practical possibilities for fruitful co-operation in this respect between countries, on a regional basis or otherwise, should be encouraged and technical assistance should be provided by international bodies, including the International Labour Office, to aid the developing countries.

9. At the planning stage of the survey as well as during the field work it is advisable to secure the collaboration of interested groups such as employers', workers' and consumer organisations, and also to widely publicise at the appropriate time the objectives of the survey with a view to ensuring public co-operation, a high response rate and general acceptance of the results.

10. Since within the context of a general survey it may not be possible to provide results with sufficient precision for such groups as pensioners, low wage earners, those living in economically depressed areas, small-scale farmers, agricultural wage earners, non-agricultural wage earners living in rural areas and other particular groups for whom detailed data may be needed for certain purposes, special household income and expenditure surveys referring to such groups may be required from time to time. In particular, more detailed data may be collected for specified groups than for other groups included in a general survey sample, provided that special measures are taken to identify the households to be treated in this way and that the sampling errors relating to the data for these groups fall within tolerable limits.

BASIC CONCEPTS AND DEFINITIONS

11. Depending on the particular objectives of the survey, including the kinds of data to be featured in the final results, a choice may be made among several types of survey. However, the basic concepts recommended in the following paragraphs should be applied in all types of household income and expenditure survey.

Unit of data collection

12. The statistical units for collection of data on the income and expenditure of private households or families are defined as follows:

Household : the concept of household for income and expenditure surveys should be the same as the one adopted in the World Programme of 1970 Censuses of Population. A household may be either:

(a) a one-person household, i.e. a person who makes provision for his own food and other essentials of living without combining with any other person, or

(b) multi-person household, i.e. a group of two or more persons who make some common provision for food or other essentials of living. The persons in the group may pool their incomes and have a common budget to a greater or lesser extent; they may be related or unrelated persons or a combination of both. The general criterion to be used in identifying the members of a multi-person household relates to the existence of common housekeeping arrangements.

Family : a family is defined for purposes of income and expenditure surveys as a type of household consisting of two or more persons related by blood, marriage or adoption who also satisfy the conditions of sharing the same housing unit and making common provisions for food and other essentials of living.

13. Sampling frames identifying the statistical units mentioned above are not always available and recourse must be made to frames such as housing lists, lists of addresses and so forth. Within the sample units selected from such frames, households or families as defined above should be identified for purposes of household income and expenditure surveys.

Income

14. (i) For household income and expenditure survey purposes, household income is the sum of money income and income in kind and consists of receipts which, as a rule, are of a recurring nature and accrue to the household or to individual members of the household regularly at annual or at more frequent intervals.

(ii) Household income is derived from the following main sources: employees' salaries, wages and other related receipts from employers, net income from self-employment, business profits, income from personal investments (rent, interest, dividends), royalties and commissions. For purposes of household surveys it is convenient to include as income the periodic payments received regularly from an inheritance or trust fund, alimony, pensions, annuities, scholarships, remittances and other cash assistance regularly received, and various other periodic receipts, together with social security and assimilated benefits in cash and in kind.

(iii) Household income in kind includes wage payments in kind, goods and services transfered free of charge by an enterprise (including farm) to an employee or to the household of the owner or part owner of the enterprise; it includes also the value of home produce consumed within the same household (e.g. agricultural products, livestock products). Where an employee buys from his employer, for his household's consumption, goods or services at concessionary prices and thus obtains a significant advantage, the value of these concessions may also be taken into account as income in kind. The estimated net rental value of owner-occupied housing is in principle also to be treated as income in kind and, similarly, the estimated gross rental value to the occupier of rent-free housing, whether obtained as wages in kind or otherwise.

(iv) So far as possible, in order to provide supplementary information on other receipts and financial flows in the household sector for use in making estimates for the national accounts and for other special purposes, the following items should be recorded in household income and expenditure surveys but should not be regarded as within the concept of household income even though the proceeds may sometimes be spent on consumption: receipts from sale of possessions, withdrawals from savings, lottery prizes, loans obtained, loan repayments (principal) received, windfall gains, lump-sum inheritances, maturity payments (other than annuities) received on life insurance policies, lump-sum compensation for injury and legal damages received. The general features distinguishing these particular receipts and other items excluded from income are the following: they are as a rule non-recurring (i.e. not occurring year after year) and are not regarded as income by the recipient household.

Consumption expenditure

15. (i) For household income and expenditure survey purposes, household consumption expenditure refers to all money expenditure by the household and individual members on goods intended for consumption and expenditure on services, plus the value of goods and services received as income in kind and consumed by the household or individual members of the household. Thus the value of items produced by the household and utilised in its own consumption, the net rental value of owner-occupied housing and the gross rental value of free housing occupied by the household represent part of household consumption expenditure.

(ii) Included in household consumption expenditure are payments, including sales taxes, made by the household for goods and services supplied and payments in connection with the use (consumption) of goods and services. Thus, payment by households for education, health and legal services are included. For certain purposes fees for driving permit, motor car registration and a number of similar charges should also be included in household consumption expenditure.

(iii) Household consumption expenditure excludes direct taxes, superannuation and other social security contributions, savings bank deposits, contributions to savings clubs or building societies, life insurance premiums, cash transfers to and disbursements on behalf of persons outside the household, and repayment of loans. Also excluded are disbursements in the nature of investments, gambling losses, cash grants and donations (except small contributions of a recurrent nature to churches and charitable institutions).

Household expenditure

16. Household expenditure includes consumption expenditure and non-consumption expenditure. The non-consumption expenditure of the household includes income tax and other direct taxes, pension and social security contributions and assimilated insurance premiums, remittances, gifts and similar transfers by the household as a whole and its individual members. Excluded are additions to savings, amounts invested or loaned, repayments of loans and outlays for other financial transactions. However, wherever it is both feasible and convenient to do so, information on those items also may be collected from households for use in making estimates for national accounts or for other special purposes.

BASIC METHODOLOGY

17. (i) For income and expenditure surveys, the size of the sample of households should be sufficient to ensure adequate representation of households of different sizes and compositions, income classes and socio-economic groups, as well as urban and rural areas and different climatic zones within the country. However, as noted in paragraph 10 above, supplementary surveys may be required to provide data adequate for separate analysis of these groups.

(ii) The design of the sample and the selection of sample households should be made in accordance with appropriate sampling techniques in order to obtain results as precise as possible with the resources available, taking into account the circumstances such as availability of suitable sampling frames. So far as possible, the sampling method employed should permit calculation of sampling error. Thorough research should be carried out to find and clearly identify the most suitable sampling frame, to determine the optimum stratification and other salient features of the sample to be used, as well as the best procedures for selection of the sample units.

18. In planning household income and expenditure surveys provision should be made for preliminary or pilot studies through which proposed methods and questionnaires can be tested, interviewers trained and where necessary information useful for the design of an efficient sample can be gathered. So far as possible, provision should be made in the final survey plan for systematic checks and controls designed to detect, at an early stage, errors or deficiencies in the collection of data and in the responses obtained from households, with a view to necessary remedial action.

19. (i) For the collection of details of household income and expenditure, the relative advantages of using the interview method, or the account book method, or a combination of the two, in the particular circumstances of the inquiry should be carefully investigated. Different methods of collection may be used for different components of the household account to obtain results of optimum quality.

(ii) Surveys normally should represent a full year of household accounts to take into account seasonal variation in income and expenditure.

20. (i) The choice of appropriate reference periods for collection of data on various components of the income and the expenditure of households needs to be based on careful experimentation in the practical application of the concepts and definition and investigation of respondents' ability to provide the information. Where the interview method is used, analysis of data derived in past household expenditure surveys will frequently assist in determining the optimum recall period for different types of items in the household account, as well as appropriate reference periods for reporting of the data, which have a great bearing on the quality and reliability of the data collected.

(ii) Where apparent biases due to unsatisfactory recall or reference periods are discovered in the survey results (e.g. through comparisons with other data on total consumption of particular commodities) an attempt should be made to assess the extent of the biases among particular population strata by making further investigations, such as a post-enumeration survey, or by thorough analysis of individual expenditure patterns among selected groups of households.

(iii) Similarly, apparent biases in reporting of expenditure, e.g. overstatement of consumption of luxury items or understatement of consumption of alcoholic drinks, tobacco, etc., should be thoroughly investigated with a view to assessment of their importance.

(iv) Other biases and non-sampling errors often more important than the above, especially understatement of income, may arise in particular circumstances in certain countries. When these are detected, remedial action should be taken along the lines indicated above in subparagraph (ii) or information should be provided on their nature and importance. Particular efforts should be made to correct the understatement of income by households.

21. Every effort should be made to limit to the minimum the rate of non-response and in this connection the length of the reference period chosen for the survey can be of great importance.

22. The measurement of consumption expenditure should be made on the basis of the total quantity and value of goods and services consumed by, or purchased by, or delivered to, the household. The choice of the basis on which household consumption is to be measured usually depends on whether the items of consumption are mostly purchases for cash or are derived to a large extent from home production and receipts in kind. In general, it is more appropriate in developing countries to

measure the goods and services actually consumed by households during the reference period, especially in rural areas.

23. In countries where consumption articles are mostly purchased, the measurement of household consumption expenditure should be made on the basis of the total quantity and value of the various consumption goods and services delivered to or obtained by the household during the specified period. In practice, data may often be satisfactorily collected on the value of goods and services paid for, irrespective of when delivery takes place. In using the latter basis, the quantities of goods and services paid for should also be recorded, wherever possible. Data on quantities consumed are particularly valuable for analysis of food consumption. Where there is little variation in stocks, the amounts purchased correspond with the quantities consumed.

24. (i) The quantity and the value of household consumption in the form of home produce consumed (e.g. agricultural and livestock products) and other receipts in kind should be estimated and recorded. The value according to appropriate prices (usually local retail market prices) should be entered as income and as expenditure to ensure that total food and other consumption, and the corresponding expenditures, are recorded on a comparable basis for different households.

(ii) Where retail prices are used, valuation on the alternative basis of producers' prices may also be useful for other purposes such as national accounts statistics.

(iii) If the rental value of owner-occupied housing (net) or rent-free housing (gross) is imputed, it should be estimated and entered as income in the household account. The same amount should be added to household expenditure. The amounts of housing charges paid by the owner-occupier, such as rates or community taxes on house owners, water and sewerage charges, repairs and maintenance of the dwelling, are treated as expenditure; the net rental value would not include these amounts. If the rent-free occupier of housing pays such housing charges himself, the rental value should be imputed on a net basis.

(iv) Other income in kind should be treated as recommended in subparagraphs (i) and (ii) above.

25. Important supplementary details concerning characteristics of households, their economic situation and living conditions should be collected on at least a subsample of questionnaires, whenever it is practical and desirable to do so, provided that safeguards have been taken to ensure that the quality of the basic data obtained on household income and expenditure would not be seriously affected.

CLASSIFICATIONS

26. Data on household income collected in household surveys should be classified in such a way and in such detail that it is possible to identify wages and salaries, incomes of members of producers' co-operatives, entrepreneurial income, property income and transfer income.

27. Data on household expenditure should be subdivided into consumption and non-consumption expenditures and in each case the data should be further classified in some detail. In particular, household expenditures should be reported in sufficient detail to permit their classification, so far as possible, according to the Classification of Household Goods and Services contained in the United Nations System of National Accounts (SNA, revised, 1968) and to permit their classification in other ways to meet different purposes. Details should be shown for expenditures on food, drink and tobacco, clothing and footwear, rent and fuel, furniture, household equipment and operation, medical care and health, transport and communication, recreation, education and other consumption expenditure.

TABULATION OF RESULTS

28. (i) As a rule, data obtained through household income and expenditure surveys should be tabulated in considerable detail. The following tabulations are examples:

(a) household members by sex and age group, for each type of household;

(b) households by size (number of members) and type of household (various "family nucleus" types and other households);

(c) households by main sources of income and household income group;

(d) expenditures of households on each item (or sub-group of items) of expenditure, by ranges or household income; separate data should also be given for urban and rural households respectively and, if possible, for farm households;

(e) expenditures of households according to household income, cross-classified by number of persons in the household, or by type of household;

(f) income and expenditure of households of employees and of other socio-economic groups.

(ii) It is also desirable, particularly in connection with the investigation of many aspects of levels of living of the population, to make special tabulations of household income and expenditures according to fractile groups of households. Tabulations by fractile groups are also valuable for international comparisons and comparisons over time.

29. For every group of households distinguished in tabulations of income or expenditure, the main characteristics of the households comprising the group should be indicated, giving such details as average size of household, average income per household, and the average per household of: adult males, adult females, children, persons working, persons retired and other persons unoccupied. The average number of income receivers and average number of rooms used by the household should also be indicated if possible.

30. (i) Data derived from the survey concerning food expenditure should be analysed in relation to household composition and level of living of the household (as measured by total household income or consumption expenditure) and also in relation to other significant social and economic characteristics of the household, such as type of occupation or socio-economic group of the head of household.

(ii) An analysis of quantities of foods consumed, along the same lines as indicated in the preceding subparagraph, should be undertaken wherever the data available permit.

(iii) Consumption analysis should be carried out in respect of household expenditures for certain goods (other than food) and services which have particular significance for the study of levels of living of households, such as housing, education, health, household durables and automobiles.

PRESENTATION OF RESULTS

31. Household income and expenditure survey results should be published in as much detail as is practical and compatible with keeping confidential the data furnished by individual households. Users of the data would thus be able to rearrange the data to suit their own purposes, subject to the limitations imposed by sampling variability and other factors affecting the reliability of detailed items of data.

32. (i) In addition to presenting averages covering all households in the sample, the frequency distribution should be shown for important items of data.

(ii) Wherever the simple mean is published in respect of major items or sub-groups of items concerning income, expenditure or consumption which are subject to important reservations, it is desirable that the median should also be computed and published or that some indication be given whenever the mean is subject to a large coefficient of variation.

33. (i) To assist in interpretation of the survey results, when these are published a description should also be given of the methods employed, including the sampling design and sampling methods. An indication of the variances of the sample data should be given for important items.

(ii) In the report on the household survey, information should also be given on the population universe covered by the survey, the response rate for various strata of the population, the theoretical or original sample and the effective response.

(iii) Other factors which have influenced the reliability of the survey data should also be mentioned, together with the result of any analysis made concerning the significance of non-sampling errors.

34. Full information should be given on the definitions applied and on the classifications used. If consumption scales are used, full details of their construction should be given. The methods of evaluation of income in kind and the corresponding expenditure should be described.

35. Since the quantity and value of various public and other social services (for instance, public education services, free medical services and the like) received free of charge by individual households cannot be readily evaluated, these items cannot be included in the individual household account. The report on the result of the survey should provide information (or references to sources of data) concerning such services, including, wherever possible, the total cost and number of beneficiaries and the estimated extent of consumption of the different services by the various strata of the population. Such data are essential to permit international and inter-regional comparisons of total private consumption of goods and services.

36. Services received free from other households, individuals outside the household or voluntary service organisations are also an important contribution to the level of living of some households. These services are of a voluntary nature and as a rule cannot be valued and included in the household consumption expenditure account. If possible the report on the survey should draw attention to these services, whenever appropriate.

INTERNATIONAL COMPARISONS
OF REAL WAGES [1]

6

The problem of making international comparisons of real wages was considered in 1923 by the First International Conference of Labour Statisticians, which mentioned the possibility of calculating index numbers of the purchasing power of wages by relating changes in actual earnings to changes in the cost of living and by taking the necessary precautions to ensure the comparability of the two series of data [1].

In application of a recommendation made by the First Conference, the ILO has over the years collected and published statistics of money wages, consumption and consumer prices. These data, which are specifically designed to meet the requirements of real wage comparisons, consist of hourly rates of pay or hourly earnings in a number of occupations, together with the retail prices of selected consumer goods collected in October of each year. The methods of collection and presentation of these data have been re-examined and modified several times, especially by the Second and Fourth International Conferences of Labour Statisticians (1925 and 1931). An ILO Committee of Statistical Experts established in pursuance of a resolution of the Fourth Conference continued to survey this work until the Second World War. Following the recommendations of this Committee, the Office undertook studies of the international comparison of rents, food costs and non-wage elements of remuneration.

In 1931 the ILO, while carrying out an inquiry at the request of the Ford Motor Company, investigated the problem of establishing wage differentials to compensate for differences in living costs. That inquiry was made to determine what wages would have to be paid to employees of the Company in various countries in order to provide a level of living comparable to that of its workers

---

[1] On this question reference may be made also to Ch. 3 (Wages, hours of work, labour cost and employee income) and Ch. 4 (Consumer price indices).

in Detroit. The results were published in 1932 in a volume which gives a detailed account of the methods followed in the inquiry [2]. A by-product of the inquiry was an analysis of international comparisons of food costs and rents on a theoretical and methodological basis [3]. The comparison of food costs was subsequently made the subject of a new study published in 1941 [4].

The subject of international comparisons of real wages was taken up again after the Second World War in 1954 by the Eighth International Conference of Labour Statisticians, which had before it an ILO report. This study of methods, which was revised and expanded after the Conference, is concerned with the methods whereby the different types of data relating to money wages, consumer prices and patterns of wage earners' consumption can be combined to yield a measure of real wages, i.e. of the purchasing power of money wages in terms of the goods and services which wage earners consume [5].

The resolution adopted by the Eighth Conference (see under "Text") deals with international comparisons of wages in the context of a study of relative levels of living. It defines the notion of real wages, specifies the methods of comparisons and indicates the studies and research work that should still be undertaken [6].

References

[1] ILO: *International Conference of Labour Statisticians*, Studies and reports, Series N, No. 4 (Geneva, 1924), pp. 32-34, 44, 47 and 73.

[2] — *A contribution to the study of international comparisons of costs of living*, Studies and reports, Series N, No. 17 (Geneva, 1932).

[3] — *International comparisons of cost of living* (Part I: "International comparison of food costs", by H. Staehle; and Part II: "International comparison of rents", by R. Guye), Studies and reports, Series N, No. 20 (Geneva, 1934).

[4] — *International comparisons of food costs*, by R. M. Woodbury, Studies and reports, Series N, No. 24 (Montreal, 1941).

[5] — *International comparisons of real wages*, Studies and reports, New series, No. 45 (Geneva, 1956).

[6] — *The Eighth International Conference of Labour Statisticians 1954* (Geneva, 1955; mimeographed), pp. 16-21 and 59-63).

Text

**Resolution concerning the international comparison of real wages
adopted by the Eighth International Conference of Labour Statisticians
(November-December 1954)**

The Eighth International Conference of Labour Statisticians,
. . . .
Adopts, this second day of December 1954, the following resolution:

1. International comparisons of wages are commonly used to study *(a)* the relative level of living, and *(b)* the relative cost of labour. This resolution is concerned only with comparisons of the first type.

2. Real wages are the goods and services which can be purchased with wages or are provided as wages, and must be distinguished from the broader concept of real income and the complex concept of level of living to which they are related.

3. As stated in the United Nations report on international definition and measurement of standards and levels of living (E/CN 3/179 and E/CN 5/299), no single index of the level of living can be devised to measure as a whole differences in the level of living between countries. Real wages represent one component of the level of living.

4. Comparisons of real wages may refer either to changes over time in a given place or to comparisons at a given time between places.

5. As a point of departure for the purpose of computing ratios of real wages, wages should be average earnings as defined for the present in ILO Convention No. 63 concerning statistics of wages and hours of work and the resolution concerning Convention No. 63 adopted by the Seventh International Conference of Labour Statisticians.[1]

6. The earnings should be adjusted to include social benefits, whether from employers, government or other sources. In order to take account of family allowances, separate real wage comparisons may be made for workers of different family types. Amounts of direct taxes and social insurance premiums should be deducted from earnings. The value of social benefits and payments in kind should be shown separately.

7. In comparisons not affected by important differences in consumption patterns, ratios of real wages can be computed by dividing ratios of wages expressed in terms of money by ratios of consumer prices.

8. Comparisons of real wages may relate to specified occupations or industries or may refer to broader groups of wage earners. In particular, separate real wage comparisons may be made for juveniles and females.

9. In interpreting the results of real wage comparisons, due account should be taken of the extent of unemployment.

10. Money wages may be taken as hourly or weekly earnings, provided that in either case the number of hours actually worked per week is taken into account.

11. Real wage comparisons between places should be made on the basis of the price and consumption pattern in each place. Long-run temporal comparisons should be treated analogously to spatial comparisons.

12. In addition to the methods described above, the Conference recognises the need for continuing research into methods of the international comparison of real wages, with particular reference to the comparison of disparate situations.

13. The Conference wishes to emphasise the need and feasibility of regional studies of real wages, covering groups of countries which have comparable social and economic structures, and calls the attention of the Governing Body of the International Labour Office to the resolution of the Seventh International Conference of Labour Statisticians which requested that the International Labour Office sponsor regional studies of occupational wages.

---

[1] See above, Ch. 3, "Texts", item E.

14. Where results of international wage comparisons are published, they should be accompanied by descriptions of the methods employed and by relevant supplementary information, particularly with reference to social benefits and other fringe elements of wages.

15. In view of the differences between countries in the extent to which various services are *(a)* paid for by workers out of earnings or *(b)* provided through public expenditures or by employers, the Conference emphasises the importance of further work on methods in this field.

16. In order to facilitate the international comparison of real wages, countries are urged to publish regularly the statistics of wages, hours of work, prices, and consumption essential to such comparisons, bearing in mind the resolutions of the Sixth and Seventh International Conferences of Labour Statisticians with respect to statistics of wages, consumer prices and family living studies.

17. The Conference requests the Governing Body of the International Labour Office to instruct the Office to prepare a revised edition of the report on international comparisons of real wages in the light of the Conference discussion, taking account of the need for extending the report to include consideration of differences in the methods to be employed for making real wage comparisons for different purposes.

SOCIAL SECURITY

7

The International Labour Conference adopted in 1944 a resolution on the need for developing internationally comparable social security statistics. This resolution urged the ILO to continue its efforts to that end.

The need to develop social security statistics was later considered by the Seventh International Conference of Labour Statisticians in 1949. The Conference adopted a resolution recommending studies of the cost of social security and requesting that the question of methodological problems in that field be included in the agenda of a subsequent conference.

The ILO accordingly undertook a series of inquiries into the cost of social security in a number of countries. The seventh inquiry, the results of which were published in 1972, covered the period 1964-66; the comparative tables of receipts and expenditures cover the years 1949-66; the report includes in an annex a preliminary study of the scope of the social security systems [1]. The eighth inquiry, which covers the years 1967-71, will provide for the first time information on the number of persons protected.

In 1952 the International Labour Conference adopted the Social Security (Minimum Standards) Convention (No. 102) [2]. As a result, not only was the development of social security statistics stimulated but the lack of international comparability of the data was revealed.

The Eighth International Conference of Labour Statisticians accordingly adopted in 1954 a resolution recalling the need for methodological studies in the field of social security statistics. On the basis of a report by a meeting of experts held in 1956, the ILO prepared for the Ninth International Conference of Labour Statisticians (1957), which was to consider that question, a study of the compilation and utilisation of social security statistics [3].

The Conference adopted a resolution (see under "Text") pointing out the general objectives of these statistics and making recommendations concerning the collection of statistics for the appraisal of social security systems, the utilisation of social security data for the compilation of other statistics (economic, social, demographic) and measures for promoting further development of social security statistics. Furthermore, the Conference requested that the ILO be instructed to develop a common body of statistical concepts, definitions and classifications and to prepare a standard framework for presentation of the data in order to facilitate comparisons between countries [4].

In response to that request and giving effect also to a similar wish expressed in 1959 by the Committee of Social Security Experts, the ILO drew up a minimum programme of social security statistics. That programme was submitted to the Subcommittee of Actuaries of the Committee of Experts on Social Security in 1960 and was subsequently approved by the Governing Body of the ILO. With a view to facilitating its application, the Office also prepared a scheme of social security statistical tables [5]. This scheme, which takes into account the special features of social security systems in the developing countries, should make it possible to improve the co-ordination of national statistics.

References

[1] ILO: *The cost of social security, 1949-1954* (Geneva, 1958); *1949-1957* (Geneva, 1960); *1958-1960* (Geneva, 1964); *1961-1963* (Geneva, 1967); *1964-1966* (Geneva, 1972) (trilingual publications).

[2] — Convention (No. 102) concerning minimum standards of social security, 1952, published in ILO: *Conventions and Recommendations adopted by the International Labour Conference, 1919-1966* (Geneva, 1966), pp. 811-833 (also issued separately).

[3] — *Social security statistics : development and uses*, Ninth International Conference of Labour Statisticians, Report V (Geneva, 1957; mimeographed).

[4] — *Ninth International Conference of Labour Statisticians 1957* (Geneva; mimeographed), pp. 9-16, 71-81 and 89-90.

[5] International Social Security Association: "Scheme of statistical tables for the practical application of a minimum programme of social security statistics", in *International Review on Actuarial and Statistical Problems of Social Security* (Geneva), 1962, No. 8, pp. 43 ff.

Text

Resolution concerning the development of social security statistics adopted by the Ninth International Conference of Labour Statisticians (April-May 1957)

The Ninth International Conference of Labour Statisticians,

. . . .

Considering that comprehensive and up-to-date statistics on the nature and extent of social protection afforded are an essential prerequisite for the formulation of policy, the execution of programmes and the appraisal of progress realised in the field of social security,

Considering further that the elaborate records required to be maintained for the operations of social security schemes constitute potentially important sources of wider economic and social statistics not directly needed for programme appraisal,

Believing that at present social security records in most countries are not used to the full extent of their potentialities,

Considering that the development of social security statistics in many countries has suffered from the fact that in the past adequate consideration has not been given to co-ordinating social security statistics with other national statistics,

Adopts, this third day of May 1957, the following resolution:

GENERAL OBJECTIVES

1. Each country should encourage the development of a system of social security statistics adequate to serve the following major objectives:

(a) to provide basic data for the administrative control of the social security schemes and the appraisal of their operational efficiency;

(b) to provide a basis for the appraisal of the financial structure of the schemes, for actuarial valuations and for short- and long-term forecasts;

(c) to provide a means of appraising the social security system as an instrument of social policy and in particular to provide a basis for the evaluation of the level of social security protection afforded to the various population groups;

(d) to provide general information on social security;

(e) to supply data for international comparisons in the field of social security; and

(f) to supply data from administrative and accounting records to satisfy important outside needs in the fields of labour, economic, health, demographic and other statistics.

2. While the same basic information may serve most of the objectives outlined in paragraph 1 above, this resolution bears especially on the minimum requirements of statistics for the objectives *(c)*, *(d)*, *(e)* and *(f)* of paragraph 1 above.

STATISTICS FOR THE APPRAISAL OF SOCIAL SECURITY SYSTEMS

3. For the purpose of this resolution the field of social security statistics is that covered under paragraphs 4, 5 and 6 below.

4. The social security statistics of a country should cover at least (1) the contingencies and (2) the types of schemes envisaged in international labour Convention No. 102 on social security (minimum standards), 1952, namely—

(1) contingencies relating to—

(a) medical care;

(b) sickness benefit;

(c) unemployment benefit;

(d) old-age benefit;

(e) employment injury benefit;

(f) family benefit;

(g) maternity benefit;

(h) invalidity benefit;

(i) survivors' benefit.

(2) schemes organised or supervised under national law or regulations in accordance with the following principles:

(a) social insurance, compulsory schemes as well as non-compulsory schemes; the latter within the meaning of Article 6 of Convention No. 102;

(b) public service;

(c) social assistance.

5. The statistics indicated in paragraph 4 should be supplemented by statistics of schemes covering the contingencies mentioned in paragraph 4 (1) although not organised according to the principles in paragraph 4 (2) (e.g. group insurance and pensions under private schemes; provident funds), particularly when such schemes account for a significant proportion of the social protection available.

6. In countries where the national concept of social security is wider or covers contingencies not envisaged under paragraph 4 (1) above, statistics should be compiled for such additional schemes or contingencies (e.g. benefits granted to war victims, to servicemen and ex-servicemen; assistance in case of natural catastrophes; domestic help in case of sickness and old age; housing for the disabled and for the aged; holidays with pay). Statistics of such schemes should be susceptible of separate identification.

7. (1) Statistical information should be compiled on the following items:

(a) participants;

(b) beneficiaries;

(c) benefits;

(d) expenditure and income.

(2) Where a scheme covers more than one contingency the statistics should, in so far as possible, be compiled separately for each of them.

(3) Such statistics should be compiled at regular intervals, the periodicity varying according to the different schemes and the conditions in the countries concerned. In many cases yearly statistical data may be desirable.

(4) The term "participant" is used to include, as appropriate, each of the terms "covered person", "protected person", "insured person", "contributor", etc., depending on the branch of social security and the type of organisational characteristics underlying the scheme.

(5) By the term "beneficiary" is meant the person in respect of whom social security benefit is granted, irrespective of whether he is a titular beneficiary or not. Where the size of benefits depends on the number of dependants, the number of titular beneficiaries and of dependants should be indicated separately. At intervals the number of children and of adults among such dependants should be shown separately.

(6) The statistics of participants and of beneficiaries should be classified wherever possible according to the most significant demographic characteristics, such as sex, age group and, in certain cases, marital status.

8. The statistics of participants and of beneficiaries where appropriate should permit separate identification of the economically active persons included. Economically active persons included should be classified at intervals according to occupation or industry or broad occupational or industrial group as may be appropriate. Where the contribution or benefit structure of the social security scheme is related to wages, earnings or income, breakdowns according to these characteristics are also desired.

9. (1) Where there is considerable variation in the benefits afforded to the various groups covered under the social security scheme, figures should be compiled to show the distribution of beneficiaries by size of benefit. Wherever this is not feasible or not essential, at least the average rates of benefit by case or by beneficiary should be shown.

(2) The statistics of benefit should, where appropriate, include data on benefit days (weeks), and the distribution of cases or beneficiaries according to benefit duration.

10. (1) The different items of expenditure should be presented for each scheme in sufficient detail related to the different types of benefit. Wherever appropriate, the cost of administration should be shown separately. Transfers to other schemes and to reserves should be indicated wherever applicable.

(2) The different items of income should be shown according to their source as follows:

(a) contributions of insured persons;

(b) employer contributions;

(c) special taxes allocated to social security;

(d) participation of the State;

(e) participation of other public authorities;

(f) income from capital;

(g) transfers from other social security schemes;

(h) other receipts.

(3) If the scheme under consideration implies the creation and maintenance of reserves, summary data on investments should be given.

11. In the interest of a clearer understanding of the statistics by the users, compilations of social security statistics should be accompanied by definitions of terms, an indication of the coverage, essential benefit provisions and reference period of the data, and descriptions of the methods used.

12. (1) Each country should arrange for the unified presentation of social security statistics at the national level in order to provide an adequate over-all picture of the operations of the social security system. The composite national statistics should be presented in sufficient detail to permit the presentation of items according to different principles of classification.

(2) Two major principles for the classification of social security statistics should be applied, both being essential. According to the first, the major emphasis is on the contingency covered, regardless of the administrative structure. According to the second, the chief emphasis is on the existing types of schemes and the administrative structure underlying them.

13. Social security statistics should consist not only of statistical compilations of the data for each item of information, but should also include relative measures which show relationships with relevant social, demographic and economic data, thus providing significant informative indications of the progress towards the achievement of most of the major objectives outlined in paragraph 1. Some of the more significant relative measures are indicated in the appendix to the resolution. Countries should give due consideration to the computation of the relative measures indicated there.

14. (1) Social security statistics compiled for national purposes may, subject to important reservations, also be used for international or regional comparisons.

(2) The contingencies and types of schemes covered under the international labour Convention No. 102 on social security (minimum standards), 1952, supplemented by schemes indicated in paragraph 5 (and 6 where appropriate), provide a basis for international comparisons in the field of social security.

(3) There is need for caution in making international comparisons in the field of social security. Great differences exist among countries with respect to the stage of development of each social security scheme, the institutional arrangement for the administration of the scheme, the social, demographic and economic structure of the

different countries, and other differences which may affect the comparability of the social security statistics of the countries compared.

(4) If countries provide detailed breakdowns and append methodological and other explanatory information when publishing statistics on social security, this will help to overcome some of the difficulties in international comparisons.

UTILISATION OF SOCIAL SECURITY DATA FOR OTHER STATISTICS

15. (1) Every country should fully explore the possibilities for the utilisation of social security records as sources of social, demographic, economic and other general statistics. Although statistics obtained from social security records are subject to certain important reservations, including those indicated in subparagraph (2) below, they should be recognised as forming an integral part of the national system of statistics.

(2) In the wider use of social security records due account should be taken of the limitations imposed by the coverage and other provisions governing the social security scheme. Moreover, it should be noted that the administrative and financial arrangements of the social security scheme generally condition the type and nature of the statistics which can be expected to flow from it.

16. The use which can be made of social security data in the development of general-purpose statistics will depend on the circumstances in each individual country. The following uses, however, merit particular consideration:

(a) as indicators of the number and characteristics of establishments;

(b) as a universe from which to draw samples;

(c) in the preparation of national accounts;

(d) as a source of information on employment, unemployment and underemployment;

(e) as a source of information on morbidity and invalidity;

(f) as a source of information on health service personnel, the capacity of health service institutions and other aspects of medical care directly administered under the social security scheme;

(g) as a source of statistics of industrial accidents and occupational diseases;

(h) on occasion, but sometimes within important limitations, as a source of statistics on the labour force, wages, demographic statistics and migration.

17. The following elements of social security records, in so far as they are maintained by the various schemes, are particularly useful as sources of general-purpose statistics:

(a) register of insured persons and individual records of participants;

(b) register of employers or establishments;

(c) periodic employer reports on contribution payments;

(d) individual records of beneficiaries.

18. Three general categories of statistics derived from social security sources may be distinguished, in terms of frequency of collection:

(a) current series, consisting of data obtained periodically and sufficiently up to date to be independently useful in the field under observation;

(b) benchmark data, useful particularly as a basis for projecting or correcting current series obtained from other sources;

(c) data for special studies, permitting occasional analysis in considerable detail of problems of special interest.

MEASURES FOR PROMOTING FURTHER DEVELOPMENT OF
SOCIAL SECURITY STATISTICS

19. Each country is urged to consider practical steps to overcome obstacles impeding the use of social security data in developing statistics for different purposes, including such obstacles as the use of non-standard definitions and classifications by social security agencies, changes in the scope of data, and inaccessibility of the records for statistical processing.

20. Remedial measures to cope with obstacles mentioned in paragraph 19 should include—

(a) steps to stimulate interest on the part of social security administrators and potential users of social security data;

(b) allocation to social security agencies, under appropriate circumstances, of funds for statistical purposes;

(c) advance planning for the use of such data at the time social security schemes are introduced, extended or revised;

(d) technical and administrative measures such as the inclusion of supplementary questions in social security forms and the requiring of duplicate report forms for statistical use.

21. Full advantage should be taken of the technique of sampling, as a practical means of studying social security data which is still too often neglected. Not only simple sampling procedures such as systematic sampling may be used but also more complicated methods; especially in the latter case expert advice should be sought in the application of sampling procedures.

22. The problems of concepts, definitions of terms and classification in statistics in the field of social security are of a twofold nature. Firstly, there are terms of special significance in the field of social security statistics for which common national definitions are generally lacking, and secondly, there are other terms common to statistics derived from social security sources and to social and economic statistics obtained from other sources for which such national definitions do generally exist. Countries should endeavour firstly to develop, so far as possible, a national nomenclature of the terms with comparable definitions to be used by the various social security agencies in the country; secondly, countries should develop measures to reduce to a minimum the divergencies in the concepts, definitions and classifications of common interest to social security agencies and to national statistical agencies.

23. In the development and application of consistent concepts, definitions and classifications full consideration should be given to existing international standards recommended by appropriate bodies. The following international classifications are especially relevant to statistics in the field of social security and conformity with them is considered to be particularly desirable:

(a) the International Standard Industrial Classification of All Economic Activities;

(b) the International Standard Classification of Occupations;

(c) the Standard Age Intervals Recommended by the Population Commission for Census and Related Purposes;

(d) the International Statistical Classification of Diseases, Injuries and Causes of Death; also the Special List of 50 Causes for Tabulation of Morbidity for Social Security Purposes.

24. To aid in accomplishing the objectives outlined in this resolution, and particularly to promote the development of consistent concepts, definitions and classifications, each country should develop an appropriate mechanism to co-ordinate—

(a) the statistics of different social security agencies among themselves;

(b) statistics based on social security data with other relevant social, demographic and economic statistics compiled in the country.

25. In developing the co-ordinating mechanism in a country, due account should be taken of the general nature of the country's administrative structure, the number and dispersion of its social security agencies, and arrangements previously existing for co-ordination of statistical activities.

APPENDIX: TYPICAL EXAMPLES OF RELATIVE MEASURES IN SOCIAL SECURITY

A. Extent of social security coverage

The number of participants as percentage of the relevant population groups, e.g. gainfully occupied population, employed population, number employed in a given industry, etc.

B. Incidence and severity of contingency

Sickness; unemployment

(i) The number of new beneficiaries or cases during a given period, e.g. a year, as percentage of the average number of participants.

(ii) The number of benefit days (or weeks) during a given period divided by the average number of participants.

(iii) The average number of benefit days (or weeks) per case, e.g. per case terminated during a given period.

Old age

The number of old-age pensioners classified by appropriate age groups, related to the total population in the corresponding age groups.

Employment injury[1]

Relative measures to be used in employment injury statistics have already been dealt with on an international basis where frequency and severity rates for industrial injuries are concerned.

C. Level of benefits

(i) The total amount of benefits for a given period divided by the number of benefit days (or weeks).

(ii) The average rate of benefit as percentage of the appropriate average wages, earnings or income.

D. Economic incidence of social security

Expenditure for social security as percentage of national income or of consumption expenditure.

E. Trends in real per capita expenditure for social security

Expenditure for social security throughout the years divided by the number of total population, economically active population, participants, etc., and the results deflated by an appropriate price indicator.

---

[1] See also Ch. 8 (Employment injuries).

EMPLOYMENT INJURIES

8

The subject of industrial accident statistics was placed on the agenda of the First International Conference of Labour Statisticians (1923), for which the ILO had prepared a report on methods of compiling such statistics [1]. The Conference adopted a resolution covering the classification of accidents and the form of calculation of frequency and severity rates. The Conference also considered the topic of statistics of occupational diseases, requesting that they be compiled in separate tables [2].

The ILO subsequently carried out studies of the method followed in the compilation of industrial accident statistics in various sectors, including in particular coal mining and railways and then agriculture, mining and quarrying, manufacturing and railways [3, 4, 5], as well as methodological studies of statistics of occupational morbidity and mortality [6].

It appeared from the attempts made to ensure international comparability in the field of industrial accident statistics that the resolution adopted by the First International Conference of Labour Statisticians needed revision, particularly in respect of the methods used to calculate industrial injury rates. The subject was accordingly included in the agenda of the Sixth Conference (1947), for which the ILO had prepared a report on the subject [7]. The Conference adopted a resolution (see "Texts", item A) superseding the resolution of the First Conference and making detailed recommendations on the methods to be followed in calculating frequency and severity rates [8].

Some years later, in 1954, the Eighth International Conference of Labour Statisticians considered the standardisation of statistics of occupational diseases, a subject that had been treated in a report prepared by the ILO [9, 10]. The Conference adopted a resolution (see "Texts", item B) indicating in particular the sources of data to be used, the diseases to be recorded and the classifications to be established.

At the request of the Ninth International Conference of Labour Statisticians, which had noted in 1957 that the international recommendations in this field had been largely overtaken by events, the subject of industrial accident statistics was included in the agenda of the Tenth Conference in 1962. That Conference had before it a report based on the conclusions of a committee of experts convened by the ILO in 1959 and on information obtained from the governments by means of questionnaires [11]. At the close of its proceedings, the Conference adopted a resolution (see "Texts", item C) concerning statistics of employment injuries, this expression covering industrial accidents, commuting accidents and occupational diseases. With regard to the compilation of the statistics and especially of statistics of industrial accidents, the resolution sets new international standards superseding the standards set by the First and Sixth Conferences. It defines for statistical purposes the notions of fatalities, permanent disablement and temporary disablement and suggests four classifications of accidents according to type of accident, the physical agency, the nature of the injury and the bodily location of the injury [12].

References

[1] ILO: *Methods of statistics of industrial accidents*, Studies and reports, Series N, No. 3 (Geneva, 1923).

[2] — *International Conference of Labour Statisticians*, Studies and reports, Series N, No. 4 (Geneva, 1924), pp. 49-69 and 73-76.

[3] — *Methods of compiling statistics of coal-mining accidents*, Studies and reports, Series N, No. 14 (Geneva, 1929).

[4] — *Methods of compiling statistics of railway accidents*, Studies and reports, Series N, No. 15 (Geneva, 1929).

[5] — *Industrial accident statistics*, Studies and reports, Series N, No. 22 (Geneva, 1938).

[6] — *Statistical methods for measuring occupational morbidity and mortality*, Studies and reports, Series N, No. 16 (Geneva, 1930).

[7] — *Methods of statistics of industrial injuries*, Studies and reports, New series, No. 7, Part 3 (Geneva, 1948).

[8] — *The Sixth International Conference of Labour Statisticians*, Studies and reports, New series, No. 7, Part 4 (Geneva, 1948), pp. 35-41, 50 and 63-64.

[9] — *General report on progress of labour statistics*, Eighth International Conference of Labour Statisticians, Report I, Part II: "Methods of statistics of occupational diseases" (Geneva, 1954; mimeographed), pp. 39 ff.

[10] — *The Eighth International Conference of Labour Statisticians 1954* (Geneva, 1955; mimeographed), pp. 35-36 and 56-59.

[11] — *Statistics of industrial injuries*, Tenth International Conference of Labour Statisticians, Report II (Geneva, 1962; mimeographed). A new edition of this report, which was prepared in 1970 (doc. D.17.1970/X.CIST/II/SAT), contains also the conclusions and recommendations of the Tenth Conference.

[12] — *Tenth International Conference of Labour Statisticians 1962* (Geneva; mimeographed), pp. 13-18, 37-56 and 64-65.

Texts

A. Resolution concerning industrial injury rates adopted by the Sixth International Conference of Labour Statisticians (August 1947)

. . . .

7. The severity rate should be calculated by dividing the number of working days lost (multiplied by 1,000) by the number of hours of working time of all persons covered and, where practicable, rates should be calculated for principal industries, for each sex and for age groups.

8. (1) For the purpose of computing severity rates the loss from fatal injuries and those resulting in permanent total disability should be taken as equal to the loss of 7,500 [1] working days.

(2) Severity rates for injuries resulting in permanent partial disability should be computed in terms of the scales of disability in use in the various countries.

(3) Severity rates for other injuries should be computed from the number of days of disability converted to working days by multiplying by the fraction 300/365.[1]

9. In publishing severity rates classifications should preferably be given according to the major groups of disability—death, permanent total, permanent partial and temporary total—in order to permit re-calculation of the rates on an internationally comparable basis.

10. Where the number of hours worked is not known the rates should be computed by assuming 2,400 man-hours or a standard working year of 300 days for the average full-time worker.

. . . .

B. Resolution concerning statistics of occupational diseases adopted by the Eighth International Conference of Labour Statisticians (November-December 1954)

The Eighth International Conference of Labour Statisticians,

. . . .

Recognising the importance of establishing an adequate statistical basis for the measurement and analysis of occupational hazards to the health of workers, with a view to promoting measures of health protection and aiding the appraisal of progress made in eliminating health hazards,

Realising that the development of statistics of occupational diseases on more uniform lines in the various countries would be facilitated by the adoption of a standard minimum list of occupational diseases for statistical purposes and of guiding principles to be observed in the classification and presentation of available statistics,

Adopts, this second day of December 1954, the following resolution:

1. Each country should endeavour to compile and publish periodically statistics on the numbers of cases of occupational diseases.

(1) Such statistics should be based on the records of a system of compensation for employment injuries, including occupational diseases, or on a notification system designed to inform the agency charged with protection of the health of workers in places of employment, or on any other appropriate source.

---

[1] This should be regarded as a standardised procedure and it should not be interpreted as implying the actual number of days lost.

(2) Where statistics are available from more than one source, they should be compiled separately for each such source. In addition, wherever feasible, statistics from the several sources should be combined, care being taken to avoid double enumeration.

2. In publishing the statistics of occupational diseases information should be given on the following points:

(1) the nature of the source or sources used in compiling the statistics: compensation, notification or other (noting particulars);

(2) the scope of the legislation concerned;

(3) the methods used in reporting the cases of occupational disease and in compiling the statistics.

3. (1) Whenever possible, the data relating to the number of cases of occupational disease should be presented by calendar year.

(2) Each case should preferably be classified within the reporting year in which it is first recorded, distinguishing separately those which result fatally in the same year.

(3) Where possible, especially for occupational diseases with relatively high rates of delayed fatal issue, a separate tabulation should be made of deaths from occupational diseases occurring among cases which were first reported prior to the reporting year in question.

4. (1) Occupational diseases should, wherever possible, include—

(a) all diseases in the International List of Notifiable Occupational Diseases to be proposed by the International Labour Office, after consultation with the World Health Organisation and appropriate experts, in conformity with instructions of the International Labour Conference of 1953;

(b) such additional occupational diseases as are recognised by legislation or otherwise to constitute serious problems in the individual countries.

(2) The International Labour Office is urged to review the International List referred to in subparagraph (1) (a) above for the purpose of suggesting to the countries sub-groups of the listed diseases which may be useful for statistical purposes.

5. (1) Cases of each occupational disease should be shown separately, classified by industry according to the International Standard Industrial Classification of All Economic Activities.

(2) It is recommended that special studies be undertaken from time to time to determine the number of cases of occupational disease in occupations in which particular problems are believed to exist; and that in such studies reference be made to the International Standard Classification of Occupations when it has been developed.

(3) Cases of occupational disease may also be analysed by sex and age through occasional special studies.

6. When statistics are based on compensation records, non-fatal incapacitating cases should be further classified if possible into—

(1) cases of temporary incapacity;

(2) cases of permanent incapacity.

7. Wherever possible, in the statistics based on compensation records effort should be made to distinguish cases of occupational disease from cases of accident.

8. Where the statistics are based on a notification system, a clear indication should be given with respect to each disease covered as to whether the notification is compulsory or voluntary.

9. Cases of "acute" poisoning should, in general, be distinguished from cases of "chronic" poisoning and excluded from the statistics of occupational diseases. If, due to practical considerations, the "acute" cases must be included in the tabulation of statistics of occupational diseases, their inclusion should be indicated. For the purposes of this resolution, the terms "acute" and "chronic" are defined in accordance with the International Statistical Classification of Diseases, Injuries and Causes of Death.

10. Wherever possible, in statistical tabulations of cases of poisoning the numbers of cases of skin disease should be indicated separately.

11. If resources and facilities permit, the special studies referred to in paragraph 5 above should include supplementary data or estimates on the following:

(1) the aggregate numbers of man-years of exposure to the risk of each selected occupational disease, for the purpose of computing incidence rates;

(2) for selected occupational diseases for which such information would be significant, statistics of the duration of the periods during which the cases were exposed to risk, i.e. periods of employment in the hazardous occupation or on the unhealthful process.

C. Resolution concerning statistics of employment injuries adopted by the Tenth International Conference of Labour Statisticians (October 1962)

The Tenth International Conference of Labour Statisticians,

. . . .

Recognising the importance of establishing an adequate statistical basis for the analysis and measurement of risks of injury inherent in employment for the purpose of facilitating the establishment of prevention programmes, evaluating the efficiency of applying measures and promoting the development of compensation schemes,

. . . .

Considering that the recommendation of standard terminology, definitions and concepts relating to statistics of employment injuries and of guiding rules for the classification and presentation of statistics would facilitate the development of statistics of employment injuries with a higher degree of comparability, both on the national and on the international level;

Adopts this twelfth day of October 1962 the following resolution, to replace the resolutions adopted in this field by the First and Sixth International Conferences of Labour Statisticians:

TERMINOLOGY

1. (1) Employment injuries cover all injuries resulting from accidents arising out of or in the course of employment (industrial accidents and commuting accidents) and all occupational diseases.

(2) Industrial accidents are accidents occurring at the place of work and resulting in death or personal injury.

(3) Commuting accidents are accidents occurring on the way to and from work and resulting in death or personal injury.

GENERAL

2. (1) Every country should attempt to collect statistics of employment injuries systematically; these statistics should be published regularly.

(2) For the collection and compilation of such statistics, consideration should be given to the advantages of using sampling methods.

(3) Countries where the total number of industrial accidents in the course of one year is not sufficient for a detailed statistical analysis should tabulate the data recorded for a longer period which, however, should not exceed five years.

3. (1) Where the statistics cover not only industrial accidents, but also commuting accidents, or occupational diseases, or both, the data for industrial accidents, commuting accidents and occupational diseases should be shown in separate tables.

(2) In relation to occupational diseases, each country should, wherever possible, apply the provisions recommended in the resolution concerning statistics of occupational diseases, adopted by the Eighth International Conference of Labour Statisticians.[1]

4. Where injuries to self-employed persons and family workers are included in the general statistics, the statistics of such injuries should be shown separately, if possible.

5. (1) In the presentation of statistics of employment injuries, information should be furnished on the following points:

(a) the nature of the sources of the statistics, e.g. reports rendered by establishments or labour inspectorates, social security records, claims for compensation, etc.;

(b) the scope of the statistics, particularly in respect of categories of persons, divisions of economic activity or industries, the minimum size of establishments covered by the statistics, etc.;

(c) methods of reporting injuries and of compiling statistics.

(2) Where the definitions and methods of statistical compilation differ from those referred to in this resolution, the definitions and methods used should be stated clearly, so that such information may be taken into account when international comparisons are attempted.

6. (1) The unit of enumeration should be the person killed or injured as a result of a recorded accident; where one person is the victim of two or more distinct recorded accidents during the period covered by the statistics, each accident should be counted separately, i.e. the same person would be counted twice or more.

(2) Countries should also consider the compilation of statistics relating to industrial accidents, using the event as the unit instead of the person, and should classify these data according to the number of persons involved.

CLASSIFICATIONS

7. (1) In the statistics relating to a given period, industrial accidents and commuting accidents should be classified in terms of consequences of the accident according to the following definitions, on the basis of the information available at the time of compilation of the statistics:

(a) fatalities: accidents resulting in death;

(b) permanent disablement: accidents resulting in permanent physical or mental limitation or impairment;

(c) temporary disablement: accidents resulting in incapacity for work for at least one full day beyond the day on which the accident occurred, irrespective of whether the days of incapacity were days on which the victim would otherwise have been at work;

---

[1] See above, Text B.

(d) other cases: accidents resulting in incapacity for work lasting less than the period defined under (c), and not involving permanent disablement.

(2) Where the statistics are based on notifications made at the time of, or immediately after, an accident, cases indicated in clauses (b) and (c) could be combined in a single group.

(3) Where the classifications used fail to conform to the provisions of this paragraph, the precise methods used should be stated, and, in particular, the minimum duration of incapacity for work taken into account in the definition of temporary disablement cases should be indicated.

8. Industrial accident statistics should be classified according to the industry in which the person injured was employed. The classification to be used should be the International Standard Industrial Classification of All Economic Activities or an industrial classification convertible to the international one.

9. (1) For the study of circumstances surrounding industrial accidents, these accidents should be classified according to (a) type of accident and (b) agency, using the classifications given in Annexes A and B to the present resolution.

(2) Each country should specify whether the classification according to agency refers to an agency related to the injury or to an agency related to the accident.

10. Industrial accidents should also be classified separately according to the location of the injury and to the nature of the injury, using the classifications given in Annexes C and D to the present resolution.

11. From time to time, non-fatal industrial accidents should be classified according to the duration of the resulting period of incapacity for work, using, where possible, the following periods: one full day, two days, three days, four to seven days, eight to 14 days, more than 14 days, beyond the day on which the accident occurred.

12. From time to time, special inquiries may be found useful for the purpose of classifying industrial accidents according to various other characteristics, such as sex, age, occupation, skill and experience, the day of the week and the month of the year, the time of the accident in respect of the work schedule, the size of the establishment, etc. Where industrial accidents are classified according to occupation, the classification used could be the International Standard Classification of Occupations.

COMPARATIVE MEASURES

13. Sound comparisons between periods, industries and countries can only be made if the statistics of industrial accidents are considered in conjunction with employment, hours of work, production, etc., data. For such purposes, it may be useful to resort to relative measures, such as frequency, incidence and severity rates.

14. Such rates should be computed by industry and, where possible, by sex and age group, and should be presented separately for accidents resulting in death, permanent and temporary disablement, in accordance with the definitions given in paragraph 7 above.

15. (1) The frequency rate of industrial accidents should be calculated by dividing the number of accidents (multiplied by 1,000,000) which occurred during the period covered by the statistics by the number of man-hours worked by all persons exposed to risk during that same period.[1]

---

[1] FR (Frequency rate) $= \dfrac{\text{total number of industrial accidents} \times 1{,}000{,}000}{\text{Total number of man-hours worked}}$

(2) Where the number of man-hours worked is not known, the frequency rate should be computed by converting the number of persons exposed to risk into man-hours; the methods used for this conversion should be clearly described.

16. The incidence rate of industrial accidents should be calculated by dividing the number of accidents (multiplied by 1,000) which occurred during the period covered by the statistics by the average number of workers exposed to risk during that same period.

17. The purpose of a severity rate is to give some indication of the loss in terms of periods of incapacity resulting from industrial accidents. Experience has indicated wide differences in national practices; recognising this fact, it does not appear advisable, at this stage, to recommend an international standard method of compilation of severity rates without further research.

ANNEXES

A. Classification of industrial accidents according to type of accident

This classification identifies the type of event which directly resulted in the injury, i.e. the manner in which the object or substance causing the injury enters into contact with the injured person.

1 Falls of persons
    11 Falls of persons from heights (trees, buildings, scaffolds, ladders, machines, vehicles) and into depths (wells, ditches, excavations, holes in the ground)
    12 Falls of persons on the same level

2 Struck by falling objects
    21 Slides and cave-ins (earth, rocks, stones, snow)
    22 Collapse (buildings, walls, scaffolds, ladders, piles of goods)
    23 Struck by falling objects during handling
    24 Struck by falling objects, not elsewhere classified

3 Stepping on, striking against or struck by objects, excluding falling objects
    31 Stepping on objects
    32 Striking against stationary objects (except impacts due to a previous fall)
    33 Striking against moving objects
    34 Struck by moving objects (including flying fragments and particles), excluding falling objects

4 Caught in or between objects
    41 Caught in an object
    42 Caught between a stationary object and a moving object
    43 Caught between moving objects (except flying or falling objects)

5 Over-exertion or strenuous movements
    51 Over-exertion in lifting objects
    52 Over-exertion in pushing or pulling objects
    53 Over-exertion in handling or throwing objects
    54 Strenuous movements

6 Exposure to or contact with extreme temperatures
    61 Exposure to heat (atmosphere or environment)
    62 Exposure to cold (atmosphere or environment)
    63 Contact with hot substances or objects
    64 Contact with very cold substances or objects

7 Exposure to or contact with electric current

8 Exposure to or contact with harmful substances or radiations

    81   Contact by inhalation, ingestion or absorption of harmful substances

    82   Exposure to ionising radiations

    83   Exposure to radiations other than ionising radiations

9 Other types of accident, not elsewhere classified, including accidents not classified for lack of sufficient data

    91   Other types of accident, not elsewhere classified

    92   Accidents not classified for lack of sufficient data

B. Classification of industrial accidents according to agency

This classification may be used for classifying either the agency related to the injury or the agency related to the accident.

(a) When this classification is used to classify an agency related to the injury, the items selected for coding shall be those which directly inflicted the injury without regard to their influence in initiating the event designated as the accident type (see Annex A).

(b) When this classification is used to classify an agency related to the accident, the items selected for coding shall be those which, because of their hazardous nature or condition, precipitated the event designated as the accident type (see Annex A).

1 Machines

    11   Prime-movers, except electrical motors

        111   Steam engines

        112   Internal combustion engines

        119   Others

    12   Transmission machinery

        121   Transmission shafts

        122   Transmission belts, cables, pulleys, pinions, chains, gears

        129   Others

    13   Metalworking machines

        131   Power presses

        132   Lathes

        133   Milling machines

        134   Abrasive wheels

        135   Mechanical shears

        136   Forging machines

        137   Rolling-mills

        139   Others

    14   Wood and assimilated machines

        141   Circular saws

        142   Other saws

        143   Moulding machines

        144   Overhand planes

        149   Others

    15   Agricultural machines

        151   Reapers (including combine reapers)

        152   Threshers

        159   Others

113

16 Mining machinery
   161 Under-cutters
   169 Others

19 Other machines not elsewhere classified
   191 Earth-moving machines, excavating and scraping machines, except means of transport
   192 Spinning, weaving and other textile machines
   193 Machines for the manufacture of foodstuffs and beverages
   194 Machines for the manufacture of paper
   195 Printing machines
   199 Others

2 Means of transport and lifting equipment
  21 Lifting machines and appliances
    211 Cranes
    212 Lifts and elevators
    213 Winches
    214 Pulley blocks
    219 Others

  22 Means of rail transport
    221 Inter-urban railways
    222 Rail transport in mines, tunnels, quarries, industrial establishments, docks, etc.
    229 Others

  23 Other wheeled means of transport, excluding rail transport
    231 Tractors
    232 Lorries
    233 Trucks
    234 Motor vehicles, not elsewhere classified
    235 Animal-drawn vehicles
    236 Hand-drawn vehicles
    239 Others

  24 Means of air transport

  25 Means of water transport
    251 Motorised means of water transport
    252 Non-motorised means of water transport

  26 Other means of transport
    261 Cable-cars
    262 Mechanical conveyors, except cable-cars
    269 Others

3 Other equipment
  31 Pressure vessels
    311 Boilers
    312 Pressurised containers
    313 Pressurised piping and accessories
    314 Gas cylinders
    315 Caissons, diving equipment
    319 Others

32 Furnaces, ovens, kilns
- 321 Blast furnaces
- 322 Refining furnaces
- 323 Other furnaces
- 324 Kilns
- 325 Ovens

33 Refrigerating plants

34 Electrical installations, including electric motors, but excluding electric hand tools
- 341 Rotating machines
- 342 Conductors
- 343 Transformers
- 344 Control apparatus
- 349 Others

35 Electric hand tools

36 Tools, implements and appliances, except electric hand tools
- 361 Power-driven hand tools, except electric hand tools
- 362 Hand tools, not power-driven
- 369 Others

37 Ladders, mobile ramps

38 Scaffolding

39 Other equipment, not elsewhere classified

4 Materials, substances and radiations

41 Explosives

42 Dusts, gases, liquids and chemicals, excluding explosives
- 421 Dusts
- 422 Gases, vapours, fumes
- 423 Liquids, not elsewhere classified
- 424 Chemicals, not elsewhere classified
- 429 Others

43 Flying fragments

44 Radiations
- 441 Ionising radiations
- 449 Others

49 Other materials and substances not elsewhere classified

5 Working environment

51 Outdoor
- 511 Weather
- 512 Traffic and working surfaces
- 513 Water
- 519 Others

52 Indoor
- 521 Floors
- 522 Confined quarters
- 523 Stairs

    524   Other traffic and working surfaces
    525   Floor openings and wall openings
    526   Environmental factors (lighting, ventilation, temperature, noise, etc.)
    529   Others

53 Underground

    531   Roofs and faces of mine roads and tunnels, etc.
    532   Floors of mine roads and tunnels, etc.
    533   Working-faces of mines, tunnels, etc.
    534   Mine shafts
    535   Fire
    536   Water
    539   Others

6 Other agencies, not elsewhere classified

  61 Animals

    611 Live animals
    612 Animal products

  69 Other agencies, not elsewhere classified

7 Agencies not classified for lack of sufficient data

C. Classification of industrial accidents according to the nature of the injury [1]

This list is to be used to classify only injuries resulting from industrial accidents or commuting accidents; in particular, occupational diseases are excluded.

10 Fractures (N800-N829):

Includes simple fractures; fractures with injuries to soft parts of the body (compound fractures); fractures with injuries to articulations (dislocations, etc.); fractures with internal or nerve injuries.

20 Dislocations (N830-N839):

Includes sublaxations and displacements.
Excludes fracture dislocations (10).

25 Sprains and strains (N840-N848):

Includes, unless associated with an open wound, the ruptures, tears and lacerations of muscles, tendons, ligaments and joints, as well as hernias due to over-exertion.

30 Concussions and other internal injuries (N852-N855, N860-N869, N958):

Includes, unless fractures are involved, all internal contusions, haemorrhages, lacerations, ruptures.
Excludes those injuries with fracture (10).

40 Amputations and enucleations (N871, N866-N888, N896-N898):

Includes traumatic avulsion of eye.

41 Other wounds (N850, N870, N872-N879, N880-N885, N890-N895, N900-N908):

Includes lacerations, open wounds, cuts, contusions with wounds, scalp wounds, as well as loss of nails or ears; includes wounds involving injury to nerves.
Excludes traumatic amputations, enucleations; avulsion of eye (40); compound fractures (10); burns with open wounds (60); superficial injuries (50).

---

[1] The numbers N800-N999 refer to the categories of the Manual of the International Statistical Classification of Diseases, Injuries and Causes of Death.

50 Superficial injuries (N910-N918):

Includes abrasions, scratches, blisters, bites of non-venomous insects, superficial wounds; also includes superficial injuries due to foreign bodies entering in the eye.

55 Contusions and crushings (N851, N920-N929):

Includes haemarthrosis, haematoma and bruises; contusions and crushings associated with superficial injuries.

Excludes concussions (30); contusions and crushings with fracture (10); and contusions and crushings with an open wound (41).

60 Burns (N940-N949):

Includes burns from hot objects; from fire; scalds; friction burns; radiation burns (infra-red); chemical burns (external burns only); burns with open wound.

Excludes burns due to swallowing a corrosive or caustic substance (70); sunburns (80); effects of lightning (80); burns due to electric current (82); and radiation effects other than burns (83).

70 Acute poisonings (N960-N979):

Includes the acute effects of the injection, ingestion, absorption or inhalation of toxic, corrosive or caustic substances; bites of venomous animals; asphyxiation by carbon monoxide or other toxic gases.

Excludes external chemical burns (60).

80 Effects of weather, exposure, and related conditions (N980-N989):

Includes effects of reduced temperature (frostbite); the effects of heat and insolation (heat-strokes, sun-strokes); baratrauma (effects of high altitude, decompression); the effects of lightning; sound trauma (total or partial loss of hearing as a separate injury, not a sequelae of another injury).

81 Asphyxia (N990-N991):

Includes drowning, asphyxiation or suffocation by compression, constriction or strangulation; also includes asphyxiation by suppression or reduction of oxygen in the surrounding atmosphere and asphyxiation by foreign bodies in the respiratory tract.

Excludes asphyxiation by carbon monoxide or other toxic gases (70).

82 Effects of electric currents (N992):

Includes electrocution, electrical shock and burns due to electric currents.

Excludes burns caused by hot parts of electrical appliances (60) and the effects of lightning (80).

83 Effects of radiations (N993):

Includes effects caused by X-rays, radio-active substances, ultra-violet rays, ionising radiations.

Excludes burns due to radiations (60) and sun-strokes (80).

90 Multiple injuries of different nature:

This group should be used only for cases where the injured person sustained several injuries of different nature and no injury is obviously more severe than the others. In a case of multiple injuries suffered in one accident where one of the injuries is obviously more severe than the others, then this accident should be classified in the group corresponding to the nature of the more obviously severe injury.

117

99 Other and unspecified injuries (N856, N994-N999):

This group should only be used to classify injuries which cannot be classified elsewhere, such as infections, for instance.

Includes various early complications of trauma and pathological reactions which should be classified in this group only when the nature of the antecedent injury in unknown.

D. Classification of industrial accidents according to the bodily location of the injury [1]

This classification may also be used to classify commuting accidents.

The groups relating to multiple locations should be used only to classify cases where the victim suffers from several injuries to different parts of the body and no injury obviously is more severe than the others. When in an accident which caused multiple injuries located at different parts of the body one of these injuries is obviously more severe than the others, this accident should be classified in the group corresponding to the location of the obviously more severe injury. For example, a fracture of the leg accompanied by the scratch of the hand should be classified in group 54.

1 Head
  11 Cranium region (skull, brain, scalp)
  12 Eye (including orbit and optic nerve)
  13 Ear
  14 Mouth (including lips, teeth and tongue)
  15 Nose
  16 Face, locations not classified elsewhere
  18 Head, multiple locations
  19 Head, unspecified location

2 Neck (including throat and cervical vertebrae)

3 Trunk
  31 Back (spinal column and adjoining muscles, spinal cord)
  32 Chest (ribs, sternum, internal organs of the chest)
  33 Abdomen (including internal organs)
  34 Pelvis
  38 Trunk, multiple locations
  39 Trunk, unspecified location

4 Upper limb
  41 Shoulder (including clavicle and shoulder blade)
  42 Upper arm
  43 Elbow
  44 Forearm
  45 Wrist
  46 Hand (except fingers alone)
  47 Fingers
  48 Upper limb, multiple locations
  49 Upper limb, unspecified location

---

[1] The proposed classification is limited to two digits. By adding another digit countries desiring to specify the location of the injury according to the side of the body injured may do so: (1) right side; (2) left side; (3) both sides. For example, a fracture of the right arm is classified under the number 42 (1), a sprain of the left ankle under 55 (2) and a burn of both eyes under 12 (3). However, if an additional digit is not used, injuries to both wrists, or both feet, etc., should *not* be classified into group 6 (multiple locations) but under the corresponding number for an injury to one wrist (45), or one foot (56), etc., only.

5   Lower limb
51   Hip
52   Thigh (upper leg)
53   Knee
54   Leg (lower leg)
55   Ankle
56   Foot (except toes alone)
57   Toes
58   Lower limb, multiple locations
59   Lower limb, unspecified location

6   Multiple locations
61   Head and trunk, head and one or more limbs
62   Trunk and one or more limbs
63   One upper limb and one lower limb or more than two limbs
68   Other multiple locations
69   Multiple locations, unspecified

7   General injuries
71   Circulatory system in general
72   Respiratory system in general
73   Digestive system in general
74   Nervous system in general
78   Other general injuries
79   General injuries, unspecified

This group should be used only when the functioning of an active body system has been affected without a specific injury (for example, poisoning, etc.); when the systematic damage results from an injury affecting a specific part of the body (for example, a fracture of the spinal column involving injury to the spinal cord), the location of the injury to this part of the body (in this case the spinal column) should be coded.

9   Unspecified location of injury

This group should only be used when no information is available to identify the part of the body affected.

INDUSTRIAL DISPUTES

9

The subject of statistics of industrial disputes was considered in 1926 by the Third International Conference of Labour Statisticians, for which the ILO had prepared a study on methods [1, 2].

The Conference adopted a resolution (see under "Text") defining disputes and laying down detailed principles for determining the importance of a dispute (number of establishments and number of workers involved, duration of the dispute, number of man-days lost) and for their classification (according to the matter in dispute, the result of the dispute, the method of settlement of the dispute, the industries affected, the importance of the dispute and the amount of wages lost by the dispute).

References

[1] ILO: *Methods of compiling statistics of industrial disputes*, Studies and reports, Series N, No. 10 (Geneva, 1926).

[2] — *The Third International Conference of Labour Statisticians*, Studies and reports, Series N, No. 12 (Geneva, 1926), pp. 58-85, 104-108 and 115-118.

Text

Resolution concerning statistics of industrial disputes adopted by the Third International Conference of Labour Statisticians (October 1926)

In each country statistics of industrial disputes should be compiled according to the following general principles:

1. The basic unit—the case of dispute—should be defined as a temporary stoppage of work wilfully effected by a group of workers or by one or more employers with a view to enforcing a demand. Disputes affecting several establishments should be considered as one case if they are organised or directed by one person or organisation.

It is desirable to make, as far as possible, a distinction between strikes and lockouts.

2. The statistics should relate to disputes beginning in the period under review and also, but separately, to those continuing from the previous period. The total of

these two groups of disputes represents the number of disputes in existence during the period under review.

3. The importance of the dispute should be measured by ascertaining the number of establishments and of workers involved in the dispute, the duration of the dispute, and the number of man-days lost on account of the dispute.

The number of establishments affected should be based on the technical unit as defined in censuses of industries.

The number of workers involved should be based on the vacancies caused in the establishments affected by the dispute, and calculated by taking an average of the number of vacancies each day during which the dispute lasted, or, where this is not practicable, by taking an average of the number of vacancies recorded at weekly intervals.

The duration of the dispute should be expressed as the number of working days from the date on which the dispute began in the first establishment affected to the date on which it terminated in the last one.

The number of man-days lost should be based on the number of vacancies caused by the dispute during each day of the dispute, or, where this is not practicable, by multiplying the number of days for which the dispute lasted by the average number of vacancies recorded at weekly intervals.

4. The disputes should be classified according to their principal characteristics, indicating in each case the number of establishments affected and that of man-days lost:

A. The matter in dispute. The principal criterion should be the relation of the dispute to collective bargaining, as follows:

(a) Disputes related to collective bargaining:
    (i) concerning trade unionism or refusal to conclude a collective agreement;
    (ii) concerning conditions of employment:
        (1) wages;
        (2) hours of labour;
        (3) engagement or dismissal of workers;
        (4) others.

(b) Disputes not related to collective bargaining:
    (i) sympathetic disputes;
    (ii) political disputes;
    (iii) others.

Groups *(a)* (ii) may also be classified into disputes concerning general terms of future employment and disputes concerning the interpretation of existing terms of employment.

B. The result of the disputes. Disputes should be classified according to their general result from the point of view of workers involved, as follows:

(a) disputes where the workers' demands have been entirely accepted;
(b) disputes where the workers' demands have been partially accepted;
(c) disputes where the workers' demands have been rejected;
(d) disputes where the employers' demands have been entirely accepted;
(e) disputes where the employers' demands have been partially accepted;
(f) disputes where the employers' demands have been rejected;
(g) disputes with indeterminate or unknown result.

C. The method of settlement of the disputes. Disputes should be classified according to the method of their settlement on the following lines:

(a) disputes settled by direct negotiations between the two parties;

(b) disputes settled by the medium of a third party:

    (i) through voluntary conciliation accepted by the parties to the dispute;

    (ii) through compulsory conciliation imposed by the law:

    (iii) through voluntary arbitration;

    (iv) through compulsory arbitration;

(c) disputes terminated without successful negotiations.

D. The industries affected. Disputes should be classified according to the principal industrial groups. The classification may be left to the domain of national statistics.

E. The importance of disputes. Disputes should be classified according to their importance, taking as criteria the number of establishments affected, the number of workers involved, the duration of the disputes, and the number of man-days lost:

(a) Disputes should be classified according to the number of establishments affected as follows:

    (i) disputes affecting one establishment;

    (ii) disputes affecting 2 to 10 establishments;

    (iii) disputes affecting 11 to 20 establishments;

    (iv) disputes affecting 21 to 100 establishments;

    (v) disputes affecting more than 100 establishments.

(b) The classification of disputes by the number of workers involved should be as follows:

    (i) disputes affecting less than 10 workers;

    (ii) disputes affecting 10 to 100 workers;

    (iii) disputes affecting 101 to 1,000 workers;

    (iv) disputes affecting 1,001 to 10,000 workers;

    (v) disputes affecting over 10,000 workers.

(c) The classification of disputes by their duration should be as follows:

    (i) disputes lasting less than 2 working days;

    (ii) disputes lasting from 2 to 10 working days;

    (iii) disputes lasting from 11 to 50 working days;

    (iv) disputes lasting from 51 to 100 working days;

    (v) disputes lasting over 100 working days.

(d) Disputes should be classified by the number of man-days lost as follows:

    (i) disputes involving the loss of less than 20 man-days;

    (ii) disputes involving the loss of 20 to 1,000 man-days;

    (iii) disputes involving the loss of 1,001 to 50,000 man-days;

    (iv) disputes involving the loss of 50,001 to 1,000,000 man-days;

    (v) disputes involving the loss of over 1,000,000 man-days.

F. Amount of wages lost by disputes. The wage loss caused by each dispute may be estimated by multiplying the number of man-days lost by the average daily wages of the workers affected. The classification of disputes according to the amount of wages lost may be left to the domain of national statistics.

5. For the purpose of comparing the risk of industrial disputes between different industries and countries, frequency and severity rates of disputes should be calculated.

The exposure to risk should be expressed in terms of the number of full-time workers, obtained by dividing the total number of days worked during the period by the total number of normal working days in the same period.

The frequency rate should show the number of disputes per 100,000 full-time workers. The severity rate should show the number of man-days lost per 10,000 full-time workers.

6. The above-mentioned data should be published at least yearly. It is desirable, however, that preliminary figures relating more particularly to the number of disputes should be published monthly.

COLLECTIVE AGREEMENTS

10

The subject of statistics of collective agreements was examined by the Third International Conference of Labour Statisticians (1926) on the basis of a report prepared by the Office [1, 2].

The resolution adopted by the Conference (see under "Text") contains detailed recommendations on definitions, methods of compiling the statistics and classification of the data (according to the nature of the contracting parties, the scope of application of the agreement, the subjects regulated, the duration of validity, the method of conclusion of the agreement, the industries covered and the industrial importance of the agreements). Nevertheless, very few countries have developed this branch of labour statistics, in which progress depends to some extent on the methods of trade union organisation and on labour legislation.

References

[1] ILO: *Methods of compiling statistics of collective agreements*, Studies and reports, Series N, No. 11 (Geneva, 1926).

[2] — *The Third International Conference of Labour Statisticians*, Studies and reports, Series N, No. 12 (Geneva, 1926), pp. 38-57.

Text

Resolution concerning statistics of collective agreements adopted by the Third International Conference of Labour Statisticians (October 1926)

In each country information concerning collective agreements and their principal contents should be collected and published in a summary form at appropriate intervals.

It is desirable that any statistics compiled on the basis of this information should be compiled in accordance with the following general principles:

1. The collective agreement should be defined, for the purposes of statistics, as a written agreement concluded between one or more employers or an employers' organisation on the one hand, and one or more workers' organisations of any kind

on the other, with a view to determining the conditions of individual employment and, in certain cases, to the regulation of other questions relative to employment.

2. The number of collective agreements should be recorded at annual intervals according to the following scheme:

(a) number of agreements in force at the beginning of the period of registration;

(b) number of agreements concluded during the period of registration;

(c) number of agreements expired within the period of registration;

(d) number of agreements in force at the end of the period of registration;

3. The importance of each collective agreement should be measured by ascertaining the numerical strength of the contracting parties, i.e. the number of establishments covered, the total number of workers employed in these establishments, and the number of workers covered by each agreement.

The extent to which workers are covered by collective agreements should be indicated by calculating the number of workers covered by agreements as a percentage of the total number of workers in the various industries.

4. The collective agreements, together with the number of establishments and of workers covered, should be classified according to their principal legal and social characteristics on the following lines:

A. *Nature of contracting parties.* The agreements should be classified according to the nature of the contracting parties as follows:

(a) agreements concluded between an employer and his workers;

(b) agreements concluded between one or more employers and one or more workers' organisations;

(c) agreements concluded between employers' organisations and workers' organisations.

B. *Scope of application.* The agreements should be classified according to the extent of the area in which they are applicable, as follows:

(a) shop agreements, i.e. agreements applicable to a single establishment;

(b) local agreements, i.e. agreements applicable to several or all establishments of similar kind situated in the same locality;

(c) district agreements, i.e. agreements applicable to several or all establishments of similar kind situated in several or all localities belonging to a district forming an economic or an administrative unit;

(d) national agreements, i.e. agreements applicable to several or all establishments of similar kind in several districts or in the country as a whole.

C. *Subjects regulated.* The agreements should be classified in the following two principal groups:

(a) agreements regulating individual conditions of employment only;

(b) agreements regulating—in addition to individual conditions of employment—general matters relative to employment.

In group (b) the number of agreements providing for special procedures for the enforcement of the agreement may be shown separately.

The statistics should also indicate the number of agreements which regulate each subject of importance, e.g. wages, hours of work, holidays, conditions of apprenticeship, labour exchanges, works councils, conciliation and arbitration.

D. Duration of validity. The agreements should be classified according to the period for which they are concluded, as follows:

(a) 3 months or less;

(b) 3 to 6 months;

(c) 6 months to 1 year;

(d) 1 to 2 years;

(e) 2 to 3 years;

(f) more than 3 years;

(g) indefinite period.

E. Method of conclusion. The agreements should be classified according to the method of the conclusion of the agreement and according to the method of negotiation as follows:

(a) collective agreements concluded as a consequence of an industrial dispute—

    (i) by direct negotiations;

    (ii) through the intervention of a third party.

(b) collective agreements concluded as a consequence of peaceful discussion—

    (i) by direct negotiations;

    (ii) through the intervention of a third party.

F. Industries covered. The agreements should be classified according to the principal industrial groups. The classification may be left to the domain of national statistics.

G. Industrial importance. The agreements should be classified according to their industrial importance, as defined in clause 3.

(a) Classification of agreements by the number of establishments covered:

    (i) agreements covering one establishment;

    (ii) agreements covering 2 to 20 establishments;

    (iii) agreements covering 21 to 100 establishments;

    (iv) agreements covering more than 100 establishments.

(b) Classification of agreements according to the number of workers covered:

    (i) agreements covering less than 100 workers;

    (ii) agreements covering 100 to 1,000 workers;

    (iii) agreements covering 1,001 to 10,000 workers;

    (iv) agreements covering 10,001 to 100,000 workers;

    (v) agreements covering more than 100,000 workers.

A distinction should also be made between workers who are members of the organisation which is a party to the agreement and other workers to whom the agreement applies in practice.

APPENDIX.
SUBJECTS CONSIDERED AT INTERNATIONAL CONFERENCES OF LABOUR STATISTICIANS

First Conference (Geneva, 29 October-2 November 1923):

1. Classification of industries and occupations.

2. Statistics of wages and hours of work.

3. Statistics of industrial accidents.

Second Conference (Geneva, 20-25 April 1925):

1. Cost-of-living index numbers.

2. International comparisons of real wages.

3. Classification of industries.

4. Unemployment statistics.

Third Conference (Geneva, 18-23 October 1926):

1. Methods of family budget inquiries.

2. Classification of industries.

3. Statistics of collective agreements.

4. Statistics of industrial disputes.

Fourth Conference (Geneva 20-23 May 1931):

International comparisons of real wages.

Fifth Conference (Geneva, 27 September-1 October 1937):

Convention concerning statistics of wages and hours of work.

Sixth Conference (Montreal, 4-12 August 1947):

1. Employment and payroll statistics.

2. Unemployment statistics.

3. Cost-of-living statistics.

4. Industrial accident statistics.

Seventh Conference (Geneva, 26 September-8 October 1949):

1. International Standard Classification of Occupations.

2. Wages and payroll statistics.

3. Methods of family living studies.

4. Statistics of labour productivity.

Eighth Conference (Geneva, 23 November-3 December 1954):

1. General report on the progress of labour statistics.

2. Employment and unemployment statistics.

3. International Standard Classification of Occupations: sub-groups and unit groups.

4. International comparisons of real wages and costs of living: study of methods.

Ninth Conference (Geneva, 24 April-13 May 1957):

1. General report on labour statistics.

2. International Standard Classification of Occupations: major, minor and unit groups; final draft.

3. International classification according to status.

4. Measurement of underemployment.

5. Social security statistics: development and uses.

Tenth Conference (Geneva, 2-12 October 1962):

1. General report on labour statistics.

2. Statistics of industrial accidents.

3. Statistics of hours of work.

4. Special problems in the computation of consumer price index numbers.

Eleventh Conference (Geneva, 18-28 October 1966):

1. Progress of labour statistics.

2. Statistics of labour cost.

3. Revision of the International Standard Classification of Occupations.

4. Measurement of underemployment.

Twelfth Conference (Geneva, 16-26 October 1973):

1. General review of labour statistics:

   (a) Objectives and programmes;

   (b) Basic labour statistics for economic and social development policies and planning.

2. Statistics of wages and employee income.

3. Scope, methods and uses of family expenditure surveys.